# Angels, Love, and Lost Souls

## A JOURNEY TO SICILY

CITY LIMITS
PUBLISHING

# Contents

*To my family, for always fostering my insatiable curiosity about the world, for nourishing my imagination, and for allowing me to explore, make mistakes, and learn from them.*

# PART I

*All Journeys begin someway, somehow, somewhere.*
*In Minnesota, Laura and John's dreams are crushed while Sebastian is at a checkmate.*
*In Sicily, a young boy hangs on to a family lost forever.*

# PROLOGUE

P atrons walked in and out of Inga's Café Excelsior, the very heart of a vibrant village on the southern west bank of Lake Minnetonka. The pungent aroma of freshly ground coffee and the scent of warm, freshly baked, crispy croissants, seduced the customers landing at the lakeside docks, guiding them to the rose shaped cast iron entrance doors of the coffee shop.

Under a cobalt blue summer sky, coffee mug in his hands, James Winslow sat at his preferred table of the outdoor patio-his hand-made wooden chair strategically positioned to give him full view of Water Street. James looked satisfied at the crowds walking up and down Excelsior's main boulevard. Just a few years earlier, the view could have not been more different: the once sleepy Minnesotan lakefront village had recently transformed into a vibrant and dynamic community. Long standing volunteer of the local Chamber of Commerce's team of retired executives mentoring young entrepreneurs, James felt a sense of accomplishment in thinking that maybe a little bit of that growth was linked to his passion for helping future business leaders.

As he looked at the crowd, James, noticed a young man crossing the street. The guy looked visibly nervous in his full Italian business attire-his hands firmly holding a couple of binders.

"It has to be him," James thought. He stood up from his chair and walked over to greet his client.

# CHAPTER I

*Chanhassen, Minnesota*

**M**y very first memory is of swimming in the cobalt blue waters of the Mediterranean Sea. My grandfather used to build large, wooden platforms on the rocky seashore of a small village on the east coast of Sicily. Baracchette, we called them. They were mostly temporary constructions made of scrap wood and nails with bamboo roofing to cover the guests from the sweltering Sicilian summer sun. All of my grandfather's children, including my father, would help him with the construction. The *masculi*, the men, would bring heavy timbers from the street level down to the shore, space them evenly to sketch an imaginary rectangle, and secure them to the ground with heavy rocks. Each post would be then joined to the next one by large wooden planks nailed crosswise, to create a strong external structure. Additional poles would be set inside the frame to support the flooring of the baracchetta. Meanwhile, the *fimmine*, the women, would stop by every once in a while to bring food, cold water, and occasionally bandage splinter injuries and hammered fingers. Children were allowed on the structure only once the railing was finished.

On a scorching and hazy hot summer day, the baracchette would look like majestic boats sailing on a sea of basalt cobbles and boulders shaped by millennia of heavy rains, ghastly winds, blazing summers, and massive waves. All different in shape and style, each family structure had its own unique design: details and techniques passed from one generation to the next one. I always wondered how my uncles would know the precise location where each supporting pillar should be installed. When I asked my dad, he told me that the secret could be revealed only by the head of the family to the next one – he also confessed that my preferred L-shaped rock had been *fixed* with dynamite many years earlier by his grandfather.

My family's baracchetta had always the same features: a long walkway that brought us to our own *castle* from the main street across the rocky shore, a large lounge area framed by robust railings to make sure children would not fall off the structure, a roof made of straws, and a beautiful green staircase that would lead us to the sea. During the summer, brothers, sisters, children and grandparents all mingled together drinking Chinotto or Coca Cola. Watermelons and mountain pears cooled in the waters of hidden springs fed by ancient rivers long ago concealed by streams of molten lava flowing down from Mount Etna.

The family soothed by the refreshing sea breeze, sunbathed browning their skin with olive oil, played cards and spent hours sharing old tales on that small piece of reclaimed land they considered their own-at least for a few months. Meanwhile, all of us younger kids would hunt for enigmatic and colorful sea creatures, learn how to swim or snorkel, and challenge the mighty sea waves. It was a magic dimension, that one. Everything stayed just the same, year after year. Nothing changed. Yes, kids slowly grew up, family members got engaged and then married. Some people would die, new children would join the family. But overall, that small world always seemed the same to me.

The piece of seashore my grandfather chose for our family's baracchetta, was protected from the sea waves by a half moon of tall, black, smooth lava rocks covered by green and brown seaweeds up to the sea level where small crabs, plump red anemones and translucent baby shrimp would bathe in the bright sunlight. Only a small opening between the coast line and the semicircle of rocks allowed the sea to enter our own, private lagoon.

I was one of the youngest children in the family. I remember playing safely, protected by the mighty, ancient rocks, while the older cousins would challenge the sea *sailing* on floating inflatable rafts or jumping toward what looked to me like towering walls of water. But all around me, protected by the surrounding rocks, in the safety of the inner part of the cove, the water was mostly still: I could play safely while wearing my pink, swan-shaped *salvagente*, lifejacket, regardless the conditions of the sea beyond my safety bubble.

I don't remember much of those early times of my life, but I do recall feeling that I was safe. My small, magic world would always be the same, unchanging, and full of amazing daily discoveries: colorful fish in the sea, little frogs tucked away in the underground fresh water springs, countless crabs and seashells hiding in the rocks. My enfolding fortress of lava protected me from everything: I felt strong, powerful, invincible, although so little and fragile. Nothing could break me.

6

But time eventually finds a way to slowly crawl up the brittle threads of a child's simple life. Nothing really stays the same forever. My world slowly started crumbling. People did indeed get older. Some moved out, leaving the island in search of better job opportunities. Others got engaged, then married, and eventually moved on to build their own families. When my grandfather died, my uncles, one by one, stopped helping each other build our baracchetta. With every defection, the chore became harder and harder. One day, the last of my uncles decided that it was not worth the effort and the expense anymore. Since my generation never learned the craft of building those amazing wooden structures towering over the Mediterranean waters, the old family tradition suddenly ended.

When we left the island, something broke inside of me. We moved to a new land: a place where we had no family or friends. People spoke a different language and customs were unfamiliar to us. All of a sudden, I lost my bubble of safety. It burst in a million shimmering pieces. I missed my island. I missed my friends. And most of all, I missed my little paradise by the sea.

For a long time, I longed for that feeling of safety and stillness. Eventually, I managed to become a strong woman. I left home to move to college. I found great and satisfying jobs. I purchased my first car, my first home, I found the man of my dreams. I thought I had it all. But what a fool was I. How sudden is the realization that you are not invincible. You are just another soul looking for purpose in life. Nothing else.

"I am so sorry" the OBGYN said. "I am so sorry." Four simple words to acknowledge failure, weakness, and wrong-doing. Four blows to crush my world. "Maybe next time…"

Sure. Next time. How many times have I lied to myself? How many times have I longed for a different outcome?

"There are other ways, you know? Have you thought about adoption?"

"Of course I have!" I would silently answer with eyes crying for help. Months of preparations. Endless days waiting for a call and sleepless nights waiting in an empty nursery. And when Lilly, the ray of sunshine finally touched my soul, the evil claws of destiny reached out to me once more to deprive me of my long deserved happiness by taking her away from me. All dreams are just illusions. My strength has been tested over and over.

As I hide in my bubble of warm, lavender-scented water, I look for refuge in these small ceramic walls of my bathtub as if I could still be protected by my ancient and towering, Sicilian lava rocks. Where is safety? Where is my strength? Where are my dreams of a large family? Where are the children I always wanted? Where is the world I wanted them to know and explore? I long for safety, refuge, security. This space is mine, at least for a few moments more. THIS is my world, my safe Heaven. All is in control here. Nothing can change. I am safe. I am whole.

"Laura, are you ok?" A voice coming from the other side of the bathroom door suddenly broke her dreamlike thoughts.

"Yes, John. I just need some time by myself. I'll join you in a few minutes."

# CHAPTER II

*Excelsior, Minnesota*

"Perfect timing for our *5-5-5* business meeting: 5 minutes after 5:00 p.m. on the fifth day of the week. You can't forget the time or the day! My name is James Winslow. I have been assigned to you by our regional team of retired executives. And unless you are not Sebastian and I completely made a fool of myself, it will be my privilege to help you with your business idea. Please have a seat and let me look at your business plan."

Sebastian shook James' hand, barely managing to mumble a "Thank you." His mind suddenly shifted to a different place and time. A feeling he had experienced when his Middle School Science teacher would talk about the Solar System and he would imagine himself leading a space ship to unknown, faraway worlds. "It all sounds so surreal. Like a scene coming out of a movie" he thought. Was the idea he had scribbled on a napkin a few weeks earlier going to really take life?

Italian by origin, Sebastian had travelled all over the world for work or leisure to finally land in Minnesota. He was very passionate about his job –and quite good at it. But lately he had come to question his purpose in life. Did he want to grow in his business line and become an executive? Or did he want to find his own way in the world by accomplishing something more meaningful? So many business books he had read. So many notepads filled with ideas, quotes and best practices. Sebastian had always delayed taking his first business step. Always… Until a few weeks earlier.

His best friend, George, had invited him to attend a dinner with one of his top clients. Maarten, a typical skinny Swedish-Minnesotan, 6-foot something, long blond hair combed into ponytails, androgynous features and skin so fair that it would become purple red at the first exposure to the sun, was a young successful serial entrepreneur. With slightly high pitched voice, elegant posture and sophisticated table manners, during dinner Maarten shared with Sebastian visions of fascinating technologies and Artificial Intelligence. By the end of the evening, Sebastian had become an admirer of Maarten's entrepreneurial spirit and lack of fear.

"When did you know you were ready for your first venture?" Sebastian had asked.

"You never know." Maarten replied smiling. "You just try to do your best. Start with small steps. Can you make a buck next week? Can you make fifty dollars the next one? Maybe $100 at the end of the month?"

"Ever thought about failure?" Asked Sebastian.

Maarten clasped a pair of perfectly manicured hands. "Ah! Like when you ski, always fall on your derriere, never on your face."

"What are you talking about?"

"Always fall on safe ground, Sebastian. Have a plan B. Never overexpose yourself. This way, if one idea fails -and by the way most of them do- you can move to the next one without having lost too much. As soon as you get back home write down a paragraph on your business proposition and sleep on it. The following day review it and expand on it." With an elegant handwriting, Maarten wrote a name and phone number on his business card, and gave it to Sebastian. "Call him. He volunteers for a Chamber of Commerce and he once saved *my* derriere."

"Are you ok?" asked James, his clear blue eyes piercing inquisitively through Italian style Luxottica glasses.

"Yes, I am fine. Thank you for asking," replied Sebastian gently scratching his head.

"Good. Let's go inside. My friend Inga, the owner of the Café, has always something new on her menu." James led the way inside the coffee shop. "My treat. You'll pay for my order once you get your first paying customer."

"Thank you James but I don't need anything elaborate. I'll have just a small espresso, if you don't mind."

"Is that all? Are you sure?" replied James perusing a kaleidoscopic display of colorful pastries and aromatic sandwiches.

"Yes, thank you," said Sebastian, mentally rehearsing his elevator pitch.

"Perfect," said James turning to the owner of Café Excelsior. "I guess we are ready to order, Inga. A short espresso for this young man and one hibiscus iced tea for me, thank you."

The young, purple striped hair girl smiled back. "No coffee for you today, James?"

"Oh no, thank you Inga. I need to stop drinking caffeine at lunchtime otherwise I'll be up all night working on new projects."

"Always trying to solve the problems of the world, don't you, James?" Inga smiled and started brewing the coffee.

"What can I say, Inga, I do my best!" James turned back to Sebastian. "Come with me, Sebastian. While Inga puts together our order, I'll show you something really interesting about this place."

Like a child on his first day at school, Sebastian followed his mentor passing by a tall pile of Mesoamerican burlap coffee bags marked with logos, weight information and worldwide addresses of the original coffee growers: their full load of beans ready to be roasted onsite.

James led the way back to the main room. "Have you noticed how all tables in this coffee shop are marked with a specific board game? I find it very clever. You come to the store to get a coffee, then you sit at one of the tables and you start playing with your friends or your kids. Next thing you know... you are thirsty or hungry again and you go back to the counter to buy something more. Genius!" He selected one of the tables set in the back of the room and motioned his guest to sit.

Sebastian noticed that the table selected by James had a chess board designed on it. *He is preparing for his opening move,* he thought, passing James one of his hot-from-the-printer copy of his business plan.

"Sebastian," started James "tell me about your idea, your vision, and your market size. But most of all, tell me why you think your product is going to be the best idea on the market."

*Time for my opening move*, thought Sebastian.

"James, my partner and I believe that travel can transform people and drive lives toward new, unchartered paths. When we leave the safety of our homes and communities to embark on a new journey, we open ourselves to the uncertainty of the unknown, we engage our innate sense of curiosity, and we search for unforgettable moments. Journeys can sometimes be difficult and make us feel uncomfortable. But with the right chaperon, as we open ourselves to knowing something (or someone) new, something magical happens: we learn new perspectives; we impact the lives of people we meet with; we bring that new world with us back home; we think differently; we reshape our relationships; we can move forward with a better knowledge of who we really are.

"Nice pitch Sebastian, tell me more..."

Under Inga's quiet and caring supervision, trays of coffee, tea, and freshly baked chocolate croissants joined and left the scrupulous business plan review. The young business owner had witnessed many of James' meetings and she could now forecast the outcome based upon just a few observations. Considering the number of questions, James' slightly elevated tone, and Sebastian's shaking of his legs under the table, Inga could easily conclude that the meeting was not going well.

"Sebastian," sighed James, closing his binder. "I really like how passionate you are about your business idea. That intensity definitely shows in the accuracy of the work you have presented to me."

"Thank you James." Sebastian felt cold sweat dripping down his temples.

"But, having said that," continued James, "I am afraid this business idea has all the potential for unavoidable failure. I just don't see how you can differentiate your product from your competitors."

James looked at Sebastian eye to eye -ice cold blue against Sebastian's warm earthy amber. "This venture won't succeed."

Sebastian looked down to the chess table. The image of a checkmate clearly taking shape in his mind. "Is there anything I can do to convince you otherwise?"

James removed his glasses and polished them a bit. e looked outside the window He looked outside the window and sighted. "I'll tell you what. Let's meet again next week. Convince me that I am wrong and I'll be your most fervent supporter."

"Thank you James. I won't disappoint you."

James stood up and shook Sebastian's hand "I am quite sure you are going to surprise me some way... Until next week." He waved to Inga and left the coffee shop.

Alone at his table, Sebastian didn't know what to do. He had spent so much time preparing for the meeting and was so sure that his passion would easily translate in numbers and projections that the thought of rejection had never occurred to him. He looked at his new business card. He had been so taken aback by what James had said, that he had forgotten to give it to him. As he passed the card from one finger to the other, Sebastian questioned its value. "Does it still mean much? Is it just a piece of paper? Or it could lead to something bigger, like a little chess piece on a board game?"

The card was nothing special. But every element was particularly meaningful to him. His title, Chief Explorer, was a suggestion from his close friend, Gerard. And so was the tagline "What's your Dream?"

"People are looking for a guide." Gerard had told him. "Someone who can translate their travel dreams in concrete plans. Somebody who has already been to those destinations and can suggest unique places and activities nobody has already done."

Of all the places he had been, Italy -and especially Sicily- was Sebastian's preferred destination. The card had his favorite colors, cobalt blue and gold, representing the sea and the sun of Sicily, his father's homeland. "A magic place," he had once told his friend Gerard. "A land of contradictions, strong emotions and unforgivable love. A place shaped by the veneration of new and ancient gods, thousand-year rivalries and lifelong alliances, majestic beauty and crude brutality." A sudden buzz broke his train of thought. Sebastian picked up his phone:

"Hi dreamer! How did the meeting go?" asked Maarten.

"Not very well", replied Sebastian

Maarten laughed. "Don't tell me. He listened carefully, asked many questions that you diligently answered, and then he told you that your idea sucks?"

"Well, not exactly…"

"So?"

"He told me that my idea will fail but we are meeting again next week. I need to convince him that I have the best product in the industry."

"I love him!"

"Excuse me"?

"He is a tough cookie!"

"What does that mean?"

"You didn't expect somebody to just jump on your travel bandwagon, did you?"

"Well, actually, I was hoping for a better outcome…"

"Sebastian. It is a jungle out there. You MUST be the best."

"Maarten, there is no Jungle in Minnesota. Woods, yes, but not a tropical jungle." Yet Sebastian knew Maarten was right. His eyes went back to the chess board printed on his table: his business card positioned where the black queen would be in her starting game position.

"You know what I mean, Sebastian. The survival of the fittest. The fight to reach the sun. The aim to conquer the world. You need to get the bug!"

"It is not flu season, Maarten. What bug are you talking about?"

"The entrepreneurial bug. The fever! The striving that will keep you up at night! Your counselor must have perceived that you don't have that yet."

"I don't? Would you have any suggestion on how I could get it? Any place where I could find infected individuals? Is there a dedicated area at the hospital downtown? Please do tell me."

"Is everything ok?" A concerned Inga stopped by to bring a glass of water.

Realizing that maybe he had been too loud, Sebastian gestured a silent "Thank you".

"Well, that is the thing, Sebastian," Marteen continued. "Sometimes you get it by working on your project. Sometimes it happens when you expect it least."

"What if I don't get the bug?"

"Well, in that case…"

Sebastian rolled his business card so that it stood up vertically, and moved it to the center of the chess board "I should keep my job right?"

"Yeah. I guess so."

"Thank you Maarten, now I really feel accomplished." A swift motion of a finger was enough to knock down the blue and gold card. "How do I fix this, Maarten?"

"Listen Sebastian, when I first met you, I thought you had something very special. I don't really care where you send me for my next vacation. I have been almost everywhere in the world and there are no properties my agents have not already scouted for me. What I am looking for, as a customer, is to see what you have seen on your hike to Preikestolen in Norway. I want to breathe the crisp air of Santorini while the sun melts with the cobalt blue sea at sunset. I want to smell a puffy, just-out of the oven- brioche filled with almond granite in Catania. I want to lose myself in a forest of chestnut trees while the ground trembles at the explosions of a bursting Etna volcano regurgitating falls of molten lava. I want to experience something that will change my life forever. Do you get my point?"

"Maarten, I can't be with every customer at the same time. It would be impossible. I would have to clone myself." Sebastian lifted his eyes to notice the elaborate and intricate design of the café's tin ceiling.

"That's it! You finally got it!"

"Cloning. Seriously, Maarten. You want me to clone myself?"

Inga smiled at the sight of Sebastian gently banging his head on one of her tables. "I love my little coffee shop," she thought.

"Technology, Sebastian. You can do anything you want with the aid of technology. Listen, my flight is leaving and I have got to go. I am going to send you the contact information to a friend of mine. Talk to him and tell him what I just told you. He is going to have an answer for you. Keep me posted."

"I will. Bye Maarten." Lifting his eyes from the table, Sebastian realized that a group of musicians had set their instruments on an improvised stage where a duet started playing Abba. The song was not one of the most famous hits of the Swedish band but in a land colonized by Scandinavians, everybody knew the lyrics.

When the small crowd started chanting about flying high like a bird in the sky, Sebastian knew it was time to leave and go home. Disheartened, he left that table where earlier on he thought his life would change forever. He walked toward the exit and opened the door to let another man come in. The man's deep, dark, brown eyes, looked terribly sad. "I wonder what his story is" Sebastian thought walking toward his car. "A broken heart. A sudden loss…"

The man ordered something to drink and sat at the table Sebastian had just left. He closed his eyes and covered his ears with his hands trying to shield himself from the music playing around him. When he opened his eyes again, he noticed a little business card. It was blue and gold. The card had only one, single, line of text "Gerard and Sebastian Travels: What's your dream?"

# CHAPTER III

*Chanhassen, MN*

John looked around his living room checking on familiar items that used to brighten his life. Boxes full of baby clothes and toys filled the entrance hall. A car seat, a pink portable swing and a play pen pushed up against the living room wall waiting to be delivered to a new address. "Everything is ready for tomorrow's shipment."

All had been said two weeks earlier, when a judge had given back little Lilly to her birth family. It did not matter that the birth family could not provide a safe place for her. It did not matter that the parents had been previously found consuming drugs and had to go through many months of rehabilitation. Lilly's parents were her birth family and as long as they promised to stay clean, that was enough for the judge. All the love that John and Laura had provided her during the time they had spent together as a foster family was not enough.

John picked up a picture frame from the nearby coffee table. Happy faces stared at him from a frozen moment of a happier past. All the colors of the Arboretum's tulips and daffodils were of no match for Lilly's purple dress, and Laura's bright, green eyes radiant with joy on that sunny Easter Day. That simple moment of happiness was now gone. No lullabies playing in the background. No more walks in the rose garden. No baby laughter. Not even the soothing sound of water flowing through the park's flower collection.

Water had stopped rushing from behind the bathroom door. "I need some time by myself," Laura had told him. "I want to be alone".

"Of course" he had said. His eyes mostly stating "I am alone as well, you know." Communications between them had been empty and broken since the disruption. Words had dissipated. Eyes had become accustomed to focusing on ephemeral objects to avoid looking at each other. Loving gestures of tenderness and affection had become a rarity. The loss of Lilly was a weight too heavy to bear. John knew he had to do something to break the wall that had suddenly grown between them, but he had no idea of what to do.

Craving a glass of water, he walked to the kitchen passing by a black baby grand piano where a few pages of sheet music of lullabies waited for attention. The kitchen was flawlessly clean: the result of an almost surgical removal of any crumb, stain, or baby item that could directly lead to unwanted memories. Alone, on the marble countertop, was a cook book.

"Croissants and Cornetti" whispered John picking up the book and scanning a few, random pages. *Laura bought me this cookbook to teach me how to make pastries and distinguish the Italian cornetti from their French and Austrian cousins.*

"Layers of butter make a great croissant." Laura had told him. "But only eggs and a secret ingredient can make perfect Italian cornetti – beyond eggs, of course."

"What's the secret ingredient?" John had asked, still new to Laura's passion for food and Italian traditions.

Laura had taken the book out of his hands and removed his thick black glasses. "Love." Warm lips sealing the revelation. "Unconditional, unapologetic, and untamed Italian love."

John savored that memory for a few minutes, then walked toward the bathroom. "Laura, are you ok?" He called.

"Yes, John. I just need some time by myself. I'll join you in a few minutes."

"Laura, I am going to Excelsior to get some chocolate croissants. Would you like them?"

No answer came from the other side of the bathroom door -not that he expected any. John walked to the mud room finding his way through boxes of nursery decorations waiting to be delivered to Lilly's new home, and opened his garage door. A charcoal Acura MDX greeted him. Before Lilly, there was no need for a larger car. But Laura had insisted on investing in a three-seater "Just in case. Who know how many family road trips are we going to take? Maybe I'll become a soccer mum. Or a Hockey one!"

Only a couple of miles of mostly undeveloped land, farm fields, small lakes, and woods separated the Rolling Acres subdivision from the city of Excelsior. Occasionally, wild turkeys and deer would cross the street. "I wonder how long until new developers will purchase this oasis of untouched land to build a new subdivision, a gas station or just another obnoxious water treatment plan," John thought.

He passed the large, red stone building of Excelsior Elementary School. "That would have been Lilly's school." He and Laura had dreamt about Lilly's first day of school and what she would wear. They had wondered what savvy words they would say... But that time was not to come. "Don't worry," the Social worker had told them. "A new baby will come to your door very soon. I promise".

"Maybe." Though John. But that new baby would not be Lilly.

He parked just outside Inga's Café Excelsior. On Main Street, people were enjoying a nice summer evening: long lines waiting outside the ice-cream parlor; beachgoers going back home after an afternoon spent on the lake; children looking at puppies on sale at the small pet store. The outdoor tables of the Café were full of customers reading newspapers or talking with friends.

He approached the entrance door-his mind still overcast by a thousand incoherent thoughts. As he went to open the door, a young man held the door for him and let him into the coffee shop. John looked at the man's large, amber eyes. He recognized that gloomy look. He saw those same eyes every morning in his bathroom mirror. The eyes of someone whose once great hopes were now crushed. But there was also a hint of defiance. The man was not yet defeated. His eyes shone with an inner strength that screamed, "I am not done. It is still not over."

He thanked the man and walked to the *bancone* as Laura always called the counter. She always felt that by calling the object with its Italian name, it would make the place smell and feel as if she was still in one of the coffee shops that populated Sicily, her homeland.

"May I help you?" said a young girl with small glasses, dark hair lined with a purple strike and a hipster-like dress. "Hope you are a lover of the arts. Tonight we are hosting the songwriters' showcase. Mostly new original songs. But every once a while they will sing some Abba songs too. At least the less famous ones."

"Well, that's quite an unexpected surprise" said John, forcing a smile. "I'll have four of your chocolate croissants and an iced tea."

"The croissants will be ready in a few minutes. We are just taking them out of the oven. Meanwhile, please have a seat and enjoy a few songs. I'll bring over your order shortly."

Music was coming from the other side of the room where a songwriters group was performing to raise funds in support of local art organizations. John had always admired people who had the courage to stand up and perform in front of a crowd. "It takes something special to put yourself out there and be ready to be judged," he thought walking toward the last empty table toward the back of the room.

He passed by Monopoly, Scrabble and checkers tables "How interesting. I've never noticed all the tables in the coffee shop had board games painted on their tabletops." The only empty table, tackled at the end of the room, showcased a full chess board. "Life really seems like a chess game sometimes. The gamble is always to try to figure out what Mother Nature's next big move is going to be."

The songwriter on stage started singing about two people talking together, but really not understanding each other at all. Their lives, thoughts and aspirations so different, it seemed they lived thousands of miles away although just a few feet separated them. Could they bridge the gap? Should they even try? Or should they just let go and move forward to their own separate journeys?

The songwriter portrayed the characters' emotions: their longings, their need to find a connection. Should two people remain together just because they have been together for a long time? What if their lives have moved toward a path that does not include the other one? The song ended with an open question mark. No answer was provided.

John imagined the two characters of the song finding a way to move forward together. Against all the odds.

"Here is your tea." Attentive and discrete as always, Inga had waited for the right moment to approach the table. The end of the song was just the right time. "I put your croissants in our special container. It will keep them warm for a while... Just in case you would like to stay longer and listen to a few more songs."

"Thank you so much." John forced a smile to Inga and took a sip of his tea. He looked down at the chessboard decorating his table. Life had thrown a bold move into their lives -those lives that used to be so perfect when Lilly's smile had filled their home. The loss had been devastating. But he refused to accept a failure. Maybe they were facing a check but not a hopeless checkmate. "What move can we make? One more song..."

A new artist walked to the microphone. He was extremely young compared to the other members of the guild. The master of ceremonies introduced him as the latest addition to the group. Mark Spencer had just joined the guild a few months earlier and was already considered one of the most promising songwriters of the region. The young man set his electronic violin in place and started playing.

It was a simple lullaby. Just a few unpretentious tunes supporting the most soothing voice John had ever heard. The singer was talking to a little child. Maybe his son? His little brother? The little boy had just been born and the singer was telling him all the great things he would see with his eyes and do with his hands. And most of all, he sang about all the places the child would visit. Those little legs one day would take him far away to explore new worlds, break barriers, and make friends across the seven seas. The boy's dreams would never die. And neither would his words and his songs.

John started crying. The music, the voice, the song. He felt like he, was that baby. He looked around. "Every soul in this room has been touched!"

All the people around him were the little child. They were all longing for a new adventure. A new exciting "thing". Whatever that "thing" may be for each and every one of them. As he looked at the chessboard again, he noticed a travel agent's business card. On the back of the card a simple tag line: "What's your dream?"

"Could that be the answer?" John thought. "A simple card that has been in front of my face all the time and I have not noticed at all?" John looked around. Some guests were talking to the young songwriter to tell him how he had touched their souls making them thinking about new goals in life.

"A new adventure?" Thought John. "Maybe that is what we need. Something new that could repair a broken bond... Why not."

He typed the website name on the phone and filled out a request form. "Worst case scenario, this won't work either. I have nothing to lose." He positioned the phone on the chessboard. "I made my move. Life, your turn!"

# CHAPTER IV

## *Acireale, Sicily*

"Mum! Dad! You should have seen the playground I found today! Swings and merry go rounds. Obstacles and monkey bars! But the most beautiful thing of all was the castle at the top of a high staircase. When I am there, I feel like a king. And when I look up to the sky, I can see so many beautiful birds flying up there.

I wish I had wings as well to fly with birds and butterflies, explore mountains and oceans, and go wherever I want.

But not now. I am too tired. I walked all day with my new friends. We found a playground nearby a church and they told me to wait for them. People here speak a different language but I can understand them. They talk like those RAI[1] TV stars, singers and actors we used to watch on TV. Good thing we learned some Italian!

Now I am going to sleep. Under a blanket of stars. Good night little brother. Good night big sister. Good night mum and dad."

---

[1] RAI: Italian Public TV Network available in many Mediterranean countries

# CHAPTER V

*Shorewood, MN*

Sebastian was slowly driving on Excelsior's Lake Street while mentally re-playing his meeting with James. He parked his car on the lake side of the street, just opposite to one of the latest mansions built to replace smaller and more traditional cottages that had once been the cornerstone of the city's unique lakeshore charm. The park of Excelsior Commons was waiting for him with its green and lush grass, ducklings playing on the shoreline, and sailing boats dotting the waters of Lake Minnetonka. He walked toward a secluded wooden bench set on top of a small hill overlooking the lake. Tall, old oak trees and bushes of plump hydrangeas shielding his secluded retreat.

"Definitely not what I was expecting. I thought my business plan was perfect..." Sebastian sat on the bench and let his mind embracing the sunset view. As his eyes followed a small boat sailing through the blue waters of Lake Minnetonka, he thought about the conversation he had with his father when his company had transferred him to Minnesota, and he had chosen the charming city of Excelsior as his new home.

*"Papa, it reminds me of a small Italian paese, village, with its Main Street full of unique stores, delightful restaurants, and a hip coffee shop where people can sit outside and enjoy the weather while playing cards or reading a newspaper. There is also a gigantic park where kids play soccer, two sandy beaches and a Marina."*

*"Son, are you missing the sea?"*

*"Yes, I am papa."* But even though the closest shore is miles away, the view of

24

Lake Minnetonka is so majestic that I get the next best thing. Maybe next year I'll take some sailing lessons with Gerard."

"Buzz, buzz", the phone vibrated in his pocket. "Hello?"

"Hi there, my name is Fernando Aguirre. I got your phone number from a friend of yours who told me you need my help." A strong voice peppered with a slight Latino accent. "I made an app for you. Would you have a minute?"

"Excuse me? Who are you again?" Replied Sebastian. "What app are you talking about?"

"A Travel app. Your friend was quite specific in the request."

"You made an app for me? But how? You don't even know what I need."

"I coded some basic features based upon the information I was given. Anything else can be built on top of it. The only thing I need is a couple of phones I could... use for testing purposes."

"Do you mean hack?" Sebastian smiled, starting to enjoy the twist of the conversation.

"Well, it would be a hacking job if you don't know that I am playing with your settings. But as I am already telling you that I am going to do it, we could better define it as a *test*. I'll be around in your neighborhood later this afternoon, house hunting. Could I use this phone number for my tests?"

Sebastian stood up looking around for unfamiliar faces who might be following him. "How do you know where I live?"

"Your friend."

"My friend must have a big mouth! All right, better get moving then. I'll see you at the house in a couple of hours. Meanwhile, I am texting you the second phone number you need."

A single *click* signaled the end of the conversation. "This Fernando must be a man of few words." Smiling, he walked downhill toward his car.

Sebastian had originally planned to take his best friend Gerard out for dinner to mark the beginning of his new venture. But that celebration would have to wait. Since their college days at Northern Kentucky University, Gerard and Sebastian had somehow managed to build their parallel careers together allowing them to live in the same cities. After working in different parts of the country, they had landed in Minnesota a few years earlier. The two of them couldn't be more different. Sebastian was the ultimate dreamer, noticing the best in every person: his glass was always half full –and sometimes with wine as well! Gerard, instead, was a rational, clear-cut, no frills and "somebody better be here right now to fix this!" kind of guy.

"Maybe just a simple dinner at home," he though while driving home through Galpin Rd. "Gerard will surely have a plethora of suggestions on how best to prepare for my next meeting with James ... Suggestions that I'll probably ignore, of course..."

He parked his car, closed the garage door and entered his living room. Little eclectic furniture decorated his brand-new home, into which he had invested all of his savings. Sebastian looked around his empty living room. "With time, this home will get full of memories and stories."

The screened three-season porch was Sebastian's final destination. He sat on a large wicker couch overlooking his lawn. From that secluded space, he could enjoy the view of a luscious Italian garden: a gift from the previous owner who so much loved gardening.

With a sharp click, he switched on his record player to play some Mozart music. He loved the sound of old records. So much warmer than the music coming out of modern electronics. He poured himself a glass of Italian, orange-based Amara liquor and quickly dialed Gerard's number. His call went directly to voicemail which, as he expected, was full. He tried again a few more times and when he had almost given up an annoyed voice answered back.

"I am trying to get something done, for Christ sake. Don't you have anything to do on a Friday night?" answered Gerard.

"Hello! Sebastian here." Completely ignoring his friend's gloomy disposition. "What are you doing?"

"My boss hates me, my team loathes me, my clients are driving me nuts. I'm telling you it doesn't look good. The way I see it, I may be unemployed in a month."

"You are such a drama queen." The sip of Amara filled Sebastian's nostrils with scent of oranges and spices from a thousand miles away. "Any time

26

you start a new job you go quickly through the four phases of excitement, burn out, boredom, and anger. And that usually takes you to either a new cycle or a new, more challenging job. How long do you have left to work for today?

"I am trying to kill a few last emails from one of my big clients. I think you met her once. The two of you could not stop talking to each other... She is an actress and a brilliant entrepreneur but extremely demanding."

"Come on, Gerard, we both know nobody is more demanding then you"

"I may be demanding," replied Gerard, his fingers hitting hard on the keyboard as if with each strike he could punch away his clients. "But your mood swings, your being aloof and your absolute, blind trust in people need immediate intervention. I actually talked to a friend of mine and he is going to give you a call to set up an appointment."

"So that was you?" Sebastian laughed. "You are the mysterious *friend*? And I thought I was being followed by the Godfather."

"I have no idea what are you talking about, Sebastian. Besides, I thought you hated the Godfather."

"That I surely do... Wait a minute. Somebody is knocking at the door."

"Sure, where am I supposed to go on a Friday evening, way beyond regular after working hour?"

Sebastian opened the door to find a big smile and two dark eyes crowned by short, black, curly hair waiting outside. "Hi Sebastian, I am Fernando. I was bringing my first load of belongings to my new home and decided to stop by. Hope it's not too late."

"Don't worry, Fernando, I was expecting you anyway." Sebastian started playing nervously with his hair, curling a few brown strands with his fingers. "Didn't you say you were still house hunting?"

"What can I say? I got the right deal at the right time and the perfect price. Now, let's get back to your requirements. I am going to send a text to your two phone numbers. Make sure you open the attached link as it will reprogram your phone to behave as the perfect Travel Agent."

"Excuse me?" Asked Sebastian, puzzled and wondering if he'd had too much of his orange flavored Amara liquor.

"It is very simple. Your device is going to take some time to learn what you need and want. As the Artificial Intelligence module learns, eventually your phone will behave like if it were you counseling your travelers."

Sebastian's glassy, big eyes stared at Fernando.

"Regardless how many clients you will have," continued Fernando, "the devices will act like a clone of you. And the devices will learn about your customers as well, of course. Think of the devices as a team of multiple *you* able to counsel a plethora of clients at the same time."

Fernando paused for a moment, waiting for a reaction. "Sebastian, are you ok?"

"I am just … processing."

"It is not perfect, Sebastian. I just started playing with it. Please, activate the link, let's see how your phone behaves. I'll stop by tomorrow to get your input. Would that work?"

"Absolutely, Fernando. But how can I repay you?"

"Your friend has already taken care of everything. See you tomorrow then. Need to move some more things to my new home before it gets too late. Oh! By the way, your friend told me you like Abba, so I peppered something here and there in the code. Bye"

"Bye". Sebastian followed Fernando to his large black van and then watched it drive two houses down. "Crap! Gerard," he thought and hurried to the screened porch. He picked up his phone to check if Gerard was still on the other side.

"Gerard? Are you still there?"

"All by myself..." Gerard sang with a dramatic tone.

"Guess what! Your friend just stopped by to share his solution."

"He stopped by your house? Is that professionally acceptable... Or even legal?"

"Of course. And he just lives two doors down from my house."

"That's weird. I had no idea he lived that close to you... Anyway, are you going to start seeing him regularly at his office?"

"No need to do so. I guess we are just going to do virtual checkpoints. Just to make sure that everything is working out ok."

"I am done with work," said Gerard looking at this clock. "I am. I'd be better off working during the week-end than sending out a message to the wrong contact or misspelling words on a note to my crazy boss. I'll get something dinner, then home."

"Dinner? Sure! What about pizza?" Sebastian exclaimed excited. "I had a horrible meeting with my business counselor and I need some comfort food."

"Do you even listen to what I say?" Gerard started walking toward the exit door of his office. "I'm going to have dinner. But by myself"

"Oh, come on, Gerard. I need a friend! I can meet you at Olives and Wine in Excelsior in thirty minutes. Just the time to check a few messages and drive back to the village... Please?"

"I rest my case. I know you'll drive me crazy for the rest of the afternoon if I don't say yes. All right check your emails while I get through the garage. Let me know if you got anything interesting."

"Let's see. Bills to pay, travel discounts, spam, an email from Gerard and Sebastian Travels, more bills..."

"Gerard and Sebastian Travels? Isn't that the site you launched last night? And by the way, why did you get me involved? I know absolutely nothing about travel. I just go where my agent -aka you- tells me to go."

"It is your financial acumen that I need... And maybe something else... Definitely not your travel expertise."

"Sebastian? What did you just say?"

"Shush. Not now. Let me read this email...."


*Dear Mr. Sebastian,*

*I found your business card at Inga's Café in Excelsior. I hope this message will not be an inconvenience to you. My wife and I are desperately in need of your guidance and advice. Our lives have come to a standstill and we need a new experience that could help us move forward. We would really appreciate you and your team helping us coordinating a trip to Italy as soon as possible. My wife is originally from the Eastern coast of Sicily. Her parents died a few years ago, before we met. She has not been back since she was a little girl and I would like you to help us spend some time on the island. If possible, I would like to keep it a surprise until we get to the airport. I'll leave it to your expertise to arrange as appropriate. I would also like you and your team to take care of any activity. Short excursions will be perfect. Nothing too stressful and physically demanding -We love arts, food and reading books. Finally, is there any way you could take care of our clothing? I have attached our size and measurements. Please let me know if our request is too demanding. I look forward to receiving an update with budget and plan soon.*

*Sincerely, John Berg*

"Gerard!"

"Yes, I am on my car's speakerphone, I'm not dead! No need to scream!" Gerard said. "I almost lost control of the car driving in this idiotic garage. How may turns are needed to get to the ground floor. And could the designers make the curves any more dangerous?"

"Listen! We have our first customer!"

"What?"

"Yes! Somebody found our business cards at the coffee shop and sent us a message!"

"Wait. We have business cards? For what? Since when?"

"Since this morning. I designed a prototype and printed out a sample for James, the business counselor."

"Just so that I understand. You're saying you left your sample of a business card on a table and somebody sent you an email request?"

"Yes!"

"To organize a trip to Sicily?"

"Yes!"

"You must be out of your mind."

"Why?"

"You have nothing built yet, with the exception of a demo website!"

"Nonsense, Gerard. I know everything about travel and Sicily is my homeland. Besides, I won't be alone on this business venture."

"Really? Who is with you?"

"WE are. We are a team"

"You and who?"

"The two of us"

"Us, who?"

"The two of us. Gerard and Sebastian!"

"You must be insane!" Gerard screamed and barely managed to stop the car at a red light at the busy crossing of Route 7 and 101. A driver looked at him with worried eyes.

"Oh, don't be silly. We can pull this together in an overnight"

"You..."

"WE!"

"WE need to get registered as soon as possible as an LLC. If WE mess up, WE can be sued for all we have!"

"You are so dramatic. Are you sure you are not Italian?"

"Definitely. "

"Would you like to become one?"

"Wait. What are you talking about?"

"All right, all right, this is what we are going to do. Focus on your driving. I'll draft the LLC docs and you can sign them at dinner. I'll make ravioli."

"I thought we were having pizza!"

"I am not depressed anymore. Now I am back to creative mode."

"Well, your ravioli better be good."

"You can bet. Nonna's[2] recipe. See you later."

---

2  Grandma

# PART II

*In Sicily, a boy is rescued.*
*In Minnesota, Laura is at a crossroad, Sebastian takes a boat ride to Wyzata,*
*and Gerard prepares to move in.*

# CHAPTER VI

## *Acireale, Sicily*

"**N**on c'e piu' la mezza stagione[3]" though Signora Carmela, touching the gold chain her husband had given her on their wedding day. Summer seemed to come earlier each year on the island of Sicily. Day after day, at 5:30, a,m, sharp, the devout Donna Carmela would walk from her home to church to help Don Gennaro, the Headmaster of St. Michael's Cathedral, with daily chores like checking the bells' clocks to make ensure correct marking of time, setting flowers in the chapel, organizing food and clothes donations, and collecting requests for prayers.

Once all of her tasks were completed, she would pray for a sick child or somebody in need. "Everybody has a job to do," she would say to Don Gennaro. "Some people were born doctors, other engineers. Some will grow to become priests or Heads of State... I am a *candle*. My job is to be ready all the time to pray for the sins of the World, provide a little light of hope to the disheartened, and clear the way to people who are lost."

On a typical day, Donna Carmela would choose the shortest way to church to start her own routine as soon as possible. Today was not a normal day. The Southern part of the Mediterranean Sea had become the epicenter of a humanitarian catastrophe as dozens of boats overflowing with migrant refugees attempted to cross the waters between North Africa and Sicily. The desperate souls, taken advantage of by ruthless mercenaries,

---

[3] There is no more middle season

would hopefully be rescued by military ships from Italy, Spain or Greece. Sometimes, however, the journey would end in tragedy: a boat carrying seventy refugees from The Middle East had just sunk the night before. Nobody knew how many people had perished; the Italian Navy was still looking for survivors. After watching the early morning news, Donna Carmela had decided to walk to church taking the longer route to have more time to pray for the souls of the people lost at sea. Walking slowly, she prayed in silence: her olive wood rosary clasped in her hands. Each street a prayer, each crossing a Requiem Aeternam, each cobblestone a caring thought for a soul lost at sea.

The gates of St. Michael's playground marked the end of her walk. Donna Carmela picked an old brass key from her purse and opened the wrought-iron gates forged during the Spanish domination of the island. She surveyed the playground and took mental note of improvements desperately needed: a new spigot for the fountain; paint for the slides; new flooring here and there.

"How did that shoe end up on the tower?" she wondered walking toward an intricate playset all Sunday school children loved. As she got closer to the structure, Donna Carmela realized that the shoe belonged to something more. "Gesu'!" exclaimed Donna Maria running toward the church as fast she could.

Inside the sacristy, enjoying a rare moment of quiet and silence, Don Calogero was already working at his desk reviewing the morning sermon while sipping a foamy, hot cappuccino topped with dark Swiss cocoa powder. "I better be careful not to stain this brand new white tunic or Donna Carmela is going to drive me nuts." He licked a few drops of coffee lingering on his salt and pepper mustache.

His eyes focused on the stained glass door separating his coveted retreat from the main altar. The old door, donated by a wealthy Spanish family in *exchange* for total absolution of sins in early 1800s, was made of strong Sicilian chestnut decorated with polychromatic glass scenes of St. Michael fighting a terrifying, towering dragon. For more than a century, the sun shone through the tall windows of the main chapel inflaming St. Michael's powerful sword with its shimmering rays, while thrusts of light and shadow gave life to a fearless beast preparing to strike against the mighty Saint in its endless fight against goodness.

Across the altar, heavy bronze doors led to an outside courtyard where children would play after mass. The master glassmakers had designed the stained glass doors to align perfectly with the opening at the opposite side so that the light coming from the gardens hit the dragon's ruby red eyes injecting life into the fiery beast: a daily reminder to Don Calogero that outside the safety of the Cathedral, evil was always ready to strike.

"The best time of the day," thought Don Calogero blowing air on top of his cappuccino. The puff lifted small clouds of steam from the foamy surface which slowly moved toward the glass door. Don Calogero followed with his eyes the vapors approaching the glass. The dragon's eyes, lit by the early morning sunrays coming from the side entrance, took life glowing back to Don Calogero with shining, piercing red brilliance. Suddenly, the beast's muscles started pulsing rhythmically. Slowly at first. Then faster and faster. Its scales moved back and forward as bursts of light and overpowering shadows fought against each other. Heavy steps became louder and louder. Something... Someone ... Was quickly approaching ... And screaming!

Don Calogero startled speechless at the glass door. His hands grabbing firmly his cappuccino cup like it could protect him from an upcoming assault. The dragon attempted a final jump toward St. Michael when the glass door flung open to let into the sacristy a flustered Donna Carmela. The ancient, polychromatic glass panels that so many people had admired and feared hit brutally the sacristy's walls and the glass panels shattered in thousand shimmering pieces. The eternal struggle of good and evil had come to an end. At least inside St. Michael Cathedral.

"Madonna Santa.[4] A child! There is a child sleeping on the playpen!" screamed Donna Carmela, wondering why Don Calogero would spend so much time trying to clean up coffee from his immaculate white tunic when a crisis needed his immediate attention. "You have got to come outside right

---

[4] Holy Virgin

now! God only knows what happened to that child."

"Of course, of course, Donna Carmela. Let's see what is going on." Don Calogero slowly walked outside his temporary cocoon looking dismayed at the floor covered in glass. A ruby red fragment shone back at him. One last time.

"Well, I guess we can finally get a new door." Donna Carmela commented unapologetically. "I couldn't stand that beast." She looked around quickly calculating the time needed to clean up. "You better call some big donors Don Calogero. This disaster won't be inexpensive."

Donna Carmela started walking toward the altar, then stopped and turned toward Don Calogero to point out a large coffee stain. "And next time, Don Calogero, it would be nice if you could keep your white tunic for Mass only. It will take a miracle to clean up that mess. Will you, please?"

# CHAPTER VII

### *Chanhassen, Minnesota*

"I can't believe I did it," thought John. "I filled out a travel request and shared my sorrows, sadness and hopes to a stranger… What was I thinking?" He scrolled his messages to read once again the reply received by the Gerard and Sebastian Travels agency.

*"Dear John,*

*Thank you so much for reaching out to Gerard and Sabastian Travels. We shall promptly review your request and will come back to you with a proposal in the next 48 hours.*

*Sincerely,*

*Gerard and Sebastian*

"Not a long reply," thought John. "But at least it's something." He had spent the rest of the weekend daydreaming. An answer meant that Mr. Sebastian and his team hadn't thought he'd lost his mind.

As he prepared breakfast, he wondered what the plan would be. Would they really arrange everything to send them to Sicily? Where would they stay? And what about the clothes? Would they really take care of that? When would they depart? He had been so entrenched in thinking about the trip itself that he had forgotten the main question. "What about Laura? What if she does not want to go?

"Are you ok?" said Laura walking into the kitchen. The dinner table was perfectly set up for breakfast: linens, plates, coffee, glasses full of fresh juice.

"Yes, honey, I was just thinking…" John was making scrambled eggs while thick slices of bacon sizzled inside the microwave.

"About?" Laura fixed a few stray hairs in her pony tail and walked to the cupboard to pick up a couple of coffee mugs, which she filled with hot espresso, freshly brewed by her red Italian coffee machine.

"What if we take a few days off?" Said John. "We could go up to Ely. The Blueberry Festival is something you always wanted to go see. We could go to the Festival, spend the night in the village and maybe visit the wolf and bear centers the following day. What do you think?" John walked toward Laura. He hugged her from behind and kissed her strawberry blonde hair.

"I don't know." Laura replied. She turned around, avoiding his eyes. "Work is hectic right now. And I always feel so tired…" She handed him a cup of coffee. "Maybe next month. Or next year."

John retreated and walked to the nearby window. Outside, colorful butterflies were dancing from one flower to the other. "Lilly loved looking at the butterflies." He thought. "Sure Laura, you are right. Let's take some time."

John took a sip of coffee and set the cup on the marble kitchen island. He thought about the time when they had both visited a marble store in north Minneapolis. Laura had adored that Uba Tuba slab from the first moment she had put her eyes on it. The cobalt blue speckles dotting the black stone. "They look like a million of Earth planets across the Universe." She had exclaimed.

"What if I drove you to work today?" John finally said. "It's such a beautiful morning… We could stop by Excelsior and have some old fashion doughnuts on the way to work. After work I could pick you up and we could go to the park. There is a band playing this afternoon. I'll have sandwiches and sodas ready to go in the car. What do you say?"

Laura got closer and put a hand on his shoulder. "John, I wish I could. I really do. But I'll be working late tonight… Maybe next time." Laura, picked up her wallet and car keys from the countertop. "I am so sorry. I can't stay for breakfast. Everything looks amazing. But I really have got to go to work."

"Don't worry. See you tonight then. I'll make dinner. Call me on your way home." Defeated, John sat at the kitchen table.

"I love you, John." Laura hugged him, and kissed his forehead.

"I love you too, Laura," replied John.

Laura got to the car and drove through her neighborhood. She loved her subdivision. Friendly neighbors, safe environment, two parks with playhouses, tennis courts, basketball hoops, small lakes and fountains. They even had a tiny wooden neighborhood library. "Perfect place to raise a child... If only we had a child," thought Laura.

At the intersection with Route 41, Laura stopped waiting for a break in the traffic to make her turn. It was like taking any other decision in her life. A dichotomy. Should she turn left and go to work, or turn right and take a day off? It was a decision between the safety of a scheduled day at work, or the random and unpredictable choice of embracing the unknown.

"John, he's so sweet," thought Laura, checking the rearview mirror. "I know he is trying his best to help me." A jogger came up from her left and passed in front of her car: mind focused on his rhythmic pace. Laura's eyes followed him jogging toward Minnewashta Park, a heaven of sandy beaches, clear waters and thick woods.

"A trip up north? He is right: I love nature... Maybe a stop by the boundary waters?" Any time she looked at large bodies of water her mid would always go back took her back home to Italy. "What if John asked me to take a trip to my homeland?" Laura switched on the emergency lights. She was not ready to make a decision.

Laura's parents had moved to the United States when she was young. Once settled in the new country, the family had rarely travelled back home either because of work requirements or lack of money. After graduation, Laura was too focused on building a career to think of a trip to Sicily. After a few years, her old friends and cousins had stopped contacting her. She had become a ghost or the "Lost American girl".

"When was the last time I was there? I don't remember... What would be waiting for me on the island?" Left or Right. Comfort or change.

"Change." She steered right. Excelsior was her new destination. "I'll stop by Inga's Café Excelsior. After that... Who knows?"

# CHAPTER VIII

*Acireale, Sicily*

"Mum! Dad! Today I met a new teacher! She is so nice. She thought I was hungry so she gave me some fruit and a coke. I also met with the Principal. He looked very serious and sad so I sang to him the song you taught me. He loved it! He said that I have the voice of an angel and he asked me if I would sing for him and the teacher every once in a while. I told him I would, of course. Maybe that will make them happy. They look so sad. Both of them... Ah! They also showed me my new room. It is so nice! Can't wait to show that to you. Good night mum. Good night dad. Good night little brother. Good night big sister."

# CHAPTER IX

*Shorewood, Minnesota*

S ebastian had not slept much of the week-end. He had been so focused on filling out the paperwork needed to register his LLC and setting up travel plans for his first customer. The evening had become night. The night, daylight. Monday morning found him on his living room couch. Glasses hanging from his nose. Laptop safely set on the table.

He stood up and slowly walked to the coffee pot. His Italian Bialetti coffee machine was still disassembled: its three main components–heating vessel, funnel and coffee collector- waiting patiently for action. "Dinner with Gerard was interesting." He thought while desperately searching for his Italian Illy coffee grounds hidden inside a refrigerator packed with vegetables, cheese, olives and a colorful collection of hams and salami. "Italians may have lost many battles. But they never starved," his dad had always told him. "Of both food and love" his mother would quickly add.

Making coffee had always been a "sacred" ritual for Sebastian's family. It would start with filling up the heating vessel with filtered water –"You never know what they put in the water." His mother always told him, never able to explain who "They" actually were and why they would put anything in the water. The process would then continue with the insertion of the funnel in the heating vessel making sure that no water would make its way from the vessel to the funnel –"It messes up the coffee" his mother would say, hushing him any time he would remind her that at the end of the day, it is hot boiling water steaming up the funnel that actually makes coffee.

With a small spoon, Sebastian added smooth, ground coffee to the funnel leaving a small gap on top. He then used the spoon to dig tiny trenches in the coffee - "Air allows the air to flow through the grounds and flavor the coffee with a strong aroma." He could hear his mum talking to him any time he prepared a new, fragrant, hot cup.

He checked a few emails on his phone, then called Gerard.

"What?"

"I am sorry, Gerard. We were supposed to have a nice evening and we spent most of the time arguing instead."

"Sebastian, I am telling you once and for all. I agree with your mentor. Your business has no chances of surviving."

Sebastian took a sip of coffee and walked over his screened porch. The smell of lavender was inebriating. "Are you still moving in?"

"Of course I am. Your house is larger than my apartment and definitely closer to my office."

"Any other perk you can think of?"

"Not at the moment… All right, all right. I'll admit it. It will be nice to have somebody to talk to at the end of a crazy day at work."

Sebastian smiled. "I look forward to tonight then."

"Do you still have my check to split household expenses?"

"Of course I do. Why?"

"Knowing you, you have probably no idea where you put it."

Sebastian went to his office perusing his desk and bookshelves. "Don't be silly. Of course I know where it is."

"Then tell me. Where is it?"

Sebastian quietly went upstairs to search in his bedroom and bathroom. "Come on, don't you trust me at all?"

"Not at all. Where is it?"

*Crap, not even in the garage!* thought Sebastian. "It's here. It was here all the time."

"Where exactly, Sebastian?

"It's here, Gerard. In my…"

"You are mess Sebastian. Let's see if I can help you. Repeat after me. In my b…"

"In my bath…"

"In my bedroom, Sebastian. In my bedroom!"

"Of course, Gerard, in my bedroom!"

"Not *your* bedroom, Sebastian. In *my* bedroom. I left it on the small table nearby the window."

Sebastian walked to the guest bedroom to finally find his lost treasure.

"Good Lord Sebastian, how did you manage to live by yourself all of this time?"

"I did… Someway," Sebastian smiled. "But it won't be for long now."

"All right, let's get this day started. I'll see you later tonight."

"Bye Gerard. See you tonight."

Sebastian was exhausted. He called work and took a day off. "Nothing is so urgent that it can't wait until tomorrow." He went back to sleep for a couple of hours. When he woke up, his head still hurt. "I'd better get some fresh air," he thought.

He took a quick shower, put on some shorts and a polo, and drove to Excelsior. It was still early in the morning but Water Street was already full of people strolling up and down. He had planned to get a coffee, first, but the temperature was up to a rare 80s in June: ice cream sounded like a better idea. There was a little kiosk nearby the docks. It only offered hotdogs and ice cream but it was always crowded with people. Everybody in town knew that the ice cream at the kiosk on Lake Minnetonka was the best in town. Sebastian had never tried it "Why not?" He thought.

As he was savoring his ice cream, Sebastian heard the loud sound of a boat. Steamboat Minnehaha, the floating museum, was slowly approaching. "This little town has so much to offer and I never have any time to take advantage of it," Sebastian thought. "What if…"

Sebastian started walking toward the docks. Steamboat Minnehaha had just been restored to its full beauty. At this time of the day, the boat offered a guided tour across the Minnetonka Lake to Wayzata for a couple of hours and then back to Excelsior. Sebastian paid the entrance fee and walked up to the top of the boat to enjoy the sun and the gentle breeze. The captain made a short announcement and the boat took off toward Wayzata. Sebastian checked his phone but there was no connection on the lake. "Another reason to enjoy the ride, learn about the history of the lake, and breathe some fresh air."

The top of the boat was completely empty. It had been the perfect day to break the daily routine and try something new. As the captain talked about the rise, fall and rebirth of the Minnetonka communities, Sebastian started thinking about his first customer. He had many ideas but where to start? All of a sudden, a woman came up the stairs. She did not look very well and could barely keep herself from falling downstairs. Sebastian offered her his hand and helped her to sit near him.

"I am really sorry." She said. "I am not feeling very well. I thought a bit of fresh air would help me but I almost didn't make it up here!" She adjusted her hair in a small pony tail. "Thank you so much for your help. My name is Laura." She offered her hand to Sebastian. He shook it. "It was my pleasure. My name is…"

The loud sound of the Minnehaha Steamboat's siren covered his voice and Laura did not catch his name. She was not interested in entertaining any sort of conversation so she did not ask him to repeat it. "Thank you," she replied instead. "I feel better now. Maybe this trip to Wayzata will make me feel better." Laura turned her head to the opposite direction to look at the mansions the dotted the shoreline.

Sebastian got the message. He moved closer to the railing and started taking pictures.

# PART III

*Laura finds a business card, Sebastian orders clothes, a boy treasures hope. Meanwhile, Gerard takes a "shower"*

# CHAPTER X

*Wyzata, Minnesota*

"It's so difficult to find a Café where baristas can make a really good espresso" thought Sebastian sipping from a small Italian coffee cup. "This Wayzata gem is just one of those places". The dark brown nectar was creamy, fragrant and the barista had even added a little, tiny bit of lemon zest. "Just perfect!"

Sebastian spent a few minutes at one of the tables: his newly printed business card in his hands. He liked to always have one business card with his freshly registered company name. It made it feel real. "I can start focusing on my first customer." He had some ideas on itineraries and activities, but one thing concerned him: clothing. His customer needed a full wardrobe of clothes that had to be selected, purchased and shipped to the destination. "What if he doesn't like what I choose or the shipment does not arrive on time?"

"Mamma mia!" His phone called for attention. Sebastian laughed thinking of his father's habit to translate in Sicilian the title of every song he heard. *Matruzza mia!*[5] Was one his favorite. "Hello? This is Sebastian."

"Good morning. This is Dr. Corby's office calling to schedule your appointment," answered a friendly voice.

"Dr. Corby? I am sorry," replied Sebastian. "There must be a mistake. I don't need to schedule any appointment."

---

[5]  Mamma Mia!

"Dr. Corby received a referral for consultation and I am just calling to follow up."

"I don't understand, Mr...."

"Kowalski. Nurse Kowalski."

"Mr. Kowalski, I am sorry. There must be a mistake. I don't need any consultation at the moment. Maybe a wrong phone number?"

"Perhaps. I'll talk to Dr. Corby to verify the information."

"Thank you Mr. Kowalski. By the way, what practice does Dr. Corby hold?"

"Psychology."

"Interesting," answered Sebastian trying to think who may have referred him. "Well, hope you'll find the right customer. Have a great day!"

"And you as well, sir."

*Strange. Why would I get referred for a consultation with a psychologist?* Sebastian left the coffee shop and started walking. The main street in Wayzata was breathtaking. Little shops on one side, the vast view of Lake Minnetonka on the other. Hundreds of sailing boats floating on the water.

*What a magnificent view.* He stopped to tie his shoelaces and when he stood up, he noticed a brand new store Insignia: Rob & Son, designer clothing and custom alteration. "Why not," Sebastian thought, and entered the shop.

A little bell announced Sebastian's entrance into the store. Everything looked extremely organized. The old style wooden shelves polished to shine. Gorgeous Italian marble floors. Venetian paintings –were they original oils? –all around the store. A captivating scent permeated a space showcasing many incredible clothes and fabrics perfectly organized like they belonged to an art gallery.

Sebastian thought about leaving immediately. Regardless of the kind of outfits he needed, there was no way he could afford anything made of Chinese silk, Italian leather or the softest cashmere wool he had ever felt in his hands. "Good afternoon, how may I help you?" A voice came from somewhere in the store.

"Good afternoon Mr. Rob", replied Sebastian, looking around without being able to see anybody in the store at all.

"Mr. Rob?" replied the voice.

"Yes. Are you Mr. Rob from Rob and Son?"

"Oh my!" A tall man with dark hair styled like the latest Vogue magazine and statuary male model body came out of one of the changing rooms. "No, no, you are looking for my father. I am not THAT old to be called Mr. or Sir!" He walked toward Sebastian offering his hand. "I am Robert. But you can call me Robbie. Nice to meet you".

"Robbie?" Said Sebastian, shaking Robert's smooth and perfectly manicured hand.

"Yes, Robert Junior"

"I guess I was not that wrong then?"

"Quite the opposite. The *sir* appellation was quite incorrect indeed." He winked.

"I am sorry, Robbie. My name is Sebastian"

"How nice! Like the Roman soldier who was eaten by the lions?"

"That was actually Daniel. Sebastian was chained to a tree and used as target for archery training."

"Potatoes, Potatoes. They both died as martyrs at a young age. How can I help you today?"

"Well, I have a very strange request, but I am not sure…"

"That I can satisfy your needs?"

"No, no, I am sure you have *everything* I may need. It is just…"

"You don't like my offering?"

"No, no. Everything here is amazing! And I really mean it. *Everything.*"

"Then say, it. What would be that wrong that you are not sure we can't find anything for you," said Robbie bending over to open a glass door under the marble countertop.

"Well, I think my budget may be too limited"

"Just tell me what you need and I am sure we can find an accommodation."

"I am arranging a trip for a client. He and his wife are going to Italy and I need to put together a full set of clothes for their trip. I have a budget in mind but I not sure I can afford your remarkable clothes…"

Robbie took a bottle out of what seemed to be a wine cooler. "What an interesting project. I always wanted to go to Italy." He opened a drawer to select a silver corkscrew among a collection of precious Tiffany utensils. "I have read a lot about the country but I have never been there. My sister, though, she flies to Italy all the time... I'll tell you what..." He repositioned the corkscrew in the drawer and selected a different bottle from his wine cooler: Moet & Chandon. "You sound like an interesting piece of work."

Robbie handed over a tablet to Sebastian "Our full catalog is on this ipad. Just select what you need and don't look at the prices. When you have some time, send me all measurements." He showed Sebastian how to navigate the catalog. "I pretty much make everything here in the shop and as you can see, we have plenty of fabrics and patterns. Once you complete your order I'll come back to you with a proposal in 48 hours. How does that sound?"

"It sounds great. Thank you Rob"

"Robbie"

"Robbie."

Sebastian selected all clothing items he thought the couple would need for the trip. He also requested some additional accessories like umbrellas and toiletries ... "Just in case". He found measurement information in his emails and completed all required sections in the electronic order. Meanwhile, Robbie was setting merchandise in place all around the shop while the bottle of Champagne was chilling in a silver basket full of ice.

"All done. Request submitted." Sebastian gave the tablet back to Robbie.

"Great! Now the fun part." Robbie opened the bottle of Champaign and filled two tall, baccarat glasses three-quarters up. "You must be thirsty," said Robbie. "Have a glass of the best bubbly waters on the market."

"I think that is called Champagne"

"Oh, that is just a name... like Evian, Ferrarelle, Perrier..." said Robbie

"I don't think there is any alcohol in Evian..."

"Are you a Chemistry professor now? Drink, it's hot as hell outside."

"Robbie, It's 70F"

"Exactly. This is Minnesota. And for Minnesotans, 70F feels like the 100s." Robbie gulped the full glass. "Ah! Only the best. God save the Queen!"

"The Queen? There is no queen in Minnesota."

"I am Swedish"

"Isn't God save the queen a British saying?"

"Listen to the Social Studies major graduate! God is the savior of all QUEENS!"

"What about the kings?"

"All dead: fighting some pointless war. Now, tell me more about the trip. Where exactly are you going to go?"

"Sicily"

"How marvelous. Tell me about its history."

"Well, I could talk about Sicily for hours but to recap a few thousand years of history, Sicily was founded by Sicelians, Sikanians and Elimi. It was later colonized by Greeks. Romans followed. Then a combination of Arabs, Bizantinians and Swedish."

"Ah! There is the Scandinavian link!" Robbie filled up the glasses once more. "To my ancestors who sailed to the Sicilian shores. Salut!"

"I guess!" Sebastian joined Robbie and drank some more. "Spanish followed, French ruled for a few years. Then Spanish kings took over again to be followed by French and British in a few locations. After Napoleon's Empire collapsed, the Spanish ruled until Sicily finally joined the Kingdom of Italy in late 1800"

"Wow! That was a history class!" said Robbie. "You are a man of many talents."

"Yes, Italian history is quite complicated and colorful. I could talk about it for hours… Which reminds me…" Sebastian checked his watch. He wanted to make sure he had enough time to prepare the house for Gerard's arrival. Everything had to be perfect: a clean house, some great food and maybe a few fragrant flowers. "Rob, I would love to stay longer but it's time for me to head back home."

"Leaving so soon? How sad." Robbie printed out Sebastian's request and perused it quickly. "You made some bold choices… Well, I'll see what I can do." He offered his hand to Sebastian. "Call me in a couple of days or stop in. There is more Champagne from where this one came from."

"Sure," said Sebastian shaking Robbie's hand. "Thank you so much for your help, Rob"

"Robbie. By the way, do you have a business card?"

"Yes, Robbie. Of course..." Sebastian searched in his pockets for his blue and gold small treasure. "Damn it. I lost it again." He thought. I am so sorry, I'll have to bring you one another time."

"Don't worry. I have all the information I need in your request. See ya."

"See you soon then." Sebastian walked toward the door and stopped. "Before I leave, what is this fragrance I smell all over the store?"

"Ah! That's my sister's business. She makes all of our perfumes in her French design shop."

"French design shop... Like in a French style store?"

"Oh, honey," Rob replied. "French in the sense that she actually owns a store in France... And a few flower farms as well..."

"How nice! Ciao Ciao Rob!"

On his way back home Sebastian called Gerard to let him know about his newly found clothing store in Wyzata. But his excitement was short lived.

"Sebastian, you are just wasting your time. Forget about this Travel venture thing and focus on something else. What about decorating your new home? Or maybe you could get involved in charity work. I can send you a few options."

"Gerard, trust me. I think I have something. Please believe in me. At least just a little bit."

"There are very few things I believe in, Sebastian. And some of them I learned them from your own father."

"My father? What did you learn from him?"

"A lot. You should listen to him more. For instance, he always mentioned an old Sicilian proverb."

"Si veni da muntagna pigghia a zappa e vo' vadagna?"[6]

"Oh God. No. I can't even imagine you holding a hoe. Farming is not in your DNA. Don't you remember what he told us when we graduated?"

---

[6] If the rain comes from the mountain, pick up your hoe and get back to work.

"I surdi fannu surdi, I pirpcchi fanno I pirocchi."[7]

"Exactly, Sebastian."

Sebastian parked his car and walked toward a grocery store. "I have no idea what you mean. Are you saying that I may have an infestation and that I need to cut my hair?"

"No, Sebastian. For the love of God, please grow up. What I am trying to say is that your idea will only generate a mess."

"Ah. This pineapple just smells delicious. Just wait to taste it when you get home tonight.

"Are you even listening to me?"

"Sorry, I got distracted. You know me. When I get into a grocery store I get into full sensorial mode. What did you say?"

"Never mind Sebastian. By the way, I am not going to be able to move toady. I have too much going on."

"But Gerard…"

"I'll move in on Friday, don't worry. My red carpet can wait. Now I need to get back to work. See you in a few days."

"Sure Gerard. Take your time. I'll see you on Friday, then. Ciao." Saddened, Sebastian put the pineapple back on the shelf and left the grocery store.

---

[7] "Money makes money. Lice makes lice"

# CHAPTER XI

M aybe it was a mistake. I feel like this ride to Wyzata will last an eternity.

Laura had felt sick since the time the Minnehaha Steamboat had left the dock. But it was too late to get off. She tried to focus her attention to the tales the captain shared with the passengers: the couple who lost their life by driving across the frozen lake when the ice wasn't thick enough to carry the weight of their car; the family feud between two brothers who owned half of an island each and ended with the creation of a canal separating the two properties; the rise and fall of Big Island's amusement park.

It didn't work. The sense of nausea just worsened. Laura walked to the rooftop. A man helped her getting settled on one of the benches. "Thank God somebody was there." She thought. "I might have fallen." She was thankful that the man had left her alone. "What was his name?" She hadn't heard.

From the top of the boat, Laura was able to enjoy a blue sky merging with the waters of the lake, the green islands and parks, and the beautiful mansions with docks for motor and sailing boats. "So many happy families," she thought, "so many beautiful homes to host them. Will John and I ever have a family of our own?"

The Minnehaha steamboat passed by a grandiose French manor style mansion. Its large yard, manicured to perfection, gently rolling down to the lake. Large stone steps leading from the mansion down to a round pagoda built on the lake. "John and I got married in a pagoda that looked just like that one." Laura lifted a hand to cover her eyes from the sun. "A time full of joy, happiness and dreams." Her mind went back to the time they had first met in Las Vegas, five years earlier, during a business conference.

*"May I ask what you are drinking?" His big smile was captivating. "It looks like something with bourbon but it smells like bacon, kind of smoky and topped by a fresh piece of rosemary."*

*Laura was exhausted after a day of business meetings and the last thing she was looking for, was talking to a stranger. "As they say in the South, everything tastes better with bacon." Laura smiled back. "It's a modern twist to an old fashion."*

That brief exchange had morphed in a night-long discovery of souls, chains of text messages, and gourmet after work dinners. At the end of the conference, they had decided to delay their flights back home to spend a full weekend backpacking in the Grand Canyon. By the time they had returned to Minneapolis, Laura Mancini, single daughter of Italian migrants whom cancer had both stolen to her too early, had married John Berg, orphan raised in institutions and foster homes who had channeled his feelings into creative web designing. A simple ceremony at Caesar's Palace wedding chapel had been enough. No big family event. Just the two of them. Both lonely. Both hungry for a big family. Laura walked to the back of the boat to admire the expansive, blue waters of Lake Minnetonka: sailing boats slowly making their way from one dock to the other. "A big family we are not meant to have…"

Many years earlier, Laura may have attributed her nausea to the joy of expecting a child. But the doctors had been very clear. "I am really sorry Laura … Your only options are adoption or surrogacy."

"Maybe we can't have children, but we could still try to build our own family by welcoming little lives who have no family of their own," John told her, sharing his personal journey as a foster child.

*We were happy. So naïve.*

A small boat was docking in the backyard of a Deephaven home. At the sight, small children came out from the house running downhill with their swimming gear.

*Months of foster parent peer group meetings, CPR trainings, readings and assignments. Then one day ... Our lives changed forever.*

Three hours. They only had three hours to review the mother's profile and reply back to the adoption agency. Laura was at work when the call came. "You have been selected!" an excited voice on the other side of the phone was screaming. "Excuse me?" Laura had replied, thinking somebody was joking with her.

"A mother has selected you and John to adopt her baby! She is already at the hospital in the delivery room. You only have three hours to get back to me. The baby is expected to come around 12:00 noon today. I am sending you the mother's profile information and please call me as soon as possible with your reply!" Laura still remembered printing out the thirty-three pages of profile and rushing out of the office to drive 25 miles north to John's office.

While speeding on the road, Laura had repeatedly dialed John's number: eyes carefully screening for cops. "Honey, I can't talk to you right now. I am in a meeting room full of clients." John finally replied, almost whispering.

"We've been selected!" Laura had screamed from the live voice system of her car.

"Selected? For what?" John walked out of the Board Room.

"Our baby. We have been selected by a mother. We only have three hours. Please meet me downstairs. I have the mother's profile with me. We need to review it and call back the agency."

The meeting with John, the rush to the hospital to only stop by Baby's R US to buy a car seat, the meeting with the little one's mother, the nights at the hospital, the discharge. Everything flashed back in front of her eyes like it happened just a few days ago and not three months earlier. "Remember!" the Director had told them, "Until the judge rules that Lilly is legally yours, you are just fostering this little angel. During the 90 days window, her family can claim her at any time."

*How could we not get in love with Lilly?*

They had not listened to the warnings. One day, just a few days before the final ruling, Lilly's father had come out of the blue to claim her as his own daughter. And that was it. John and Laura had driven Lilly to the adoption agency bringing with them most of her clothes and toys.

*We woke up as a family, we went to bed as heartbroken strangers.*

The Minnehaha steamboat landed in Wayzata. "Be back at this same spot in two hours." Announced the captain. "I'll be leaving with anybody who is back onboard. Anybody else will have to take a taxi back to Excelsior. No exceptions granted."

Laura walked alongside the lake shore. White sloops were challenging seagulls in a maritime dance orchestrated by a gentle breeze. "Hard to think that in a few months these same waters will be completely frozen and covered with a small colony of colorful ice-fishing houses," she thought.

A couple of children ran by Laura and suddenly crossed the main street, destination Dave and Buster's ice cream. A long line of people waiting outside the store for the chance of a free treat for "Customer appreciation day." Laura had no intention of waiting in line and walked to the close coffee shop instead. She ordered a tea and sat at a table nearby a large window overlooking the Lake Minnetonka. "The lake has been the stage for so many stories," she thought. "How many tales have never been told? How many stories will be lost forever?"

Lost. Like her little Lilly.

"Maybe John was right: change is what we need." Laura looked outside the café's window: Lake Minnetonka so vast and beautiful. "Where could we go?" On their first trip backpacking in the Grand Canyon they had promised each other to travel around the world and visit as many places as possible together and with their children.

If only there was a place that would not remind them of what they had lost forever... A place that was meaningful to both of them, and could create a new bond between them. "Maybe... I have not been back to my homeland since I left as a little girl many years ago." Laura thought. She had many memories, although quite faded. "Maybe we could go back and I could share with John what I remember... But I don't know where to start... "

She took another sip of her tea and as she looked down to the table, she noticed a small blue and gold card. Gerard and Sebastian Travels, What's Your Dream? "How... Could this be possible?" She picked up her phone and quickly typed the company's web address. She perused the site and loved it. She finally opened the profile portion and started typing.

# CHAPTER XII

"Little brother! Big sister! I met so many new friends today. We played hide and seek all day long. But I must have been too good. At some point, they lost me and I was alone again. Tomorrow I'll try to find places easier to find. This way I can play longer. Mum, daddy. I love my new home. So many beautiful paintings of children with wings. I wish I had wings like those children. This way I could fly to you any time I want. Good night mum, good night dad. Good night little brother. Good night big sister."

# CHAPTER XIII

*Chanhassen, Minnesota*

"Honey, how was your day?" said John. Puzzled at seeing Laura so upbeat ... Was she actually smiling?

"It was ok, John. I had an Ok day"

"Well, whatever happened, you sound cheery."

"I would not say cheery but hopeful"

"And ... should I interpret that as a good thing?"

A buzz signaled a new message in her inbox. Laura discretely checked her phone.

*"Thank you so much for reaching out to us. Gerard and I will personally review your request. Sincerely, Sebastian"*

She turned back to John setting the phone in her back pocket. She held John's hand and kissed him. "Yes. That is really good thing" said Laura.

# CHAPTER XIV

*Acireale, Sicily*

"Mum! Dad! I have a new room. It is full of colorful pictures, soft linens, and tall, skinny lamps. Before going to bed, I love playing with my tall toys. They are gigantic wooden figurines painted with gold and bright colors. The largest ones are a mum and a dad with their child. But there are also many angels, kings and princes. I pretend that they are real people and I make up stories. It is like watching TV. But I can decide what my people will do next. I wish you could see one of my shows! Good night mum. Good night dad. Good night little brother and big sister"

# CHAPTER XV

*Shorewood, Minnesota*

"Friday! Where has the week gone?" Sebastian thought while driving to Excelsior. In a few minutes he would meet James Winslow again. Just a week earlier, James had axed his business idea. A week later, Gerard and Sebastian Travels had a real customer … Well, actually two… Kind of. After his visit to Rob & Sons, Sebastian had received a new request. At first he thought there must have been a mistake as both requests had the same final destination and the same last name. But the first name was different.

"Leave it to the rational Gerard to put all pieces together," smiled Sebastian, husband and wife were trying to reconnect with each other. They both had the same idea and each wanted to surprise their spouse.

"It is like helping two customers with one service," Maarten had suggested. "And do not worry about your order. I know the tailors at Rob & Sons. They will find a way to help you." And that had actually been the most surprising development of the week. Robbie's estimate had come back exactly within budget range!

The only negative note of the week had been Gerard's reaction to the news of the creation of a business LLC. "I can't believe you used my contribution to house expenses to pay for business expenditures and LLC registration fees," Gerard had shouted "I have never agreed to be part of your idea, Sebastian, why on Earth did you do that?"

"Well, you have been helpful in helping me putting together all the documents I needed for the LLC and my meetings with the business counselors. I thought that by splitting the ownership with you, you would have been happy."

"Absolutely not! I don't understand anything about travel. You organize everything for me whenever I need to go anywhere. Why would I ever want to own a travel business?"

"I need your skills to keep me grounded, Gerard. I know nothing about business and financial management. I need your help"

"And that is why you forged my signature?"

"I did not *forge* your signature, I signed on your behalf"

"With a signature that looks like mine!"

"All signatures look the same on a computer"

"No they don't. You copied the signature on my check and deposited the check in the company's business account!"

"Well, consider it part of a "trust fund." It is still your money. Had I deposited the check in my account, it would just be mine."

"You are insane!" Gerard screamed. "What if we fail?"

"What if we don't?" replied Sebastian. "You will be able to retire early and enjoy the rest of your life. Maybe..."

"Maybe what?"

"You could even spend the rest of your days travelling!"

Gerard had stormed out slamming the front door and Sebastian had not heard from him since. "I am confident he will show up at the house later in the afternoon to move in. Hopefully he got over it," thought Sebastian, as he walked into Inga's Café.

James Winslow was waiting at their usual outdoor patio table.

"Coffee, James? This time I'll pay." Sebastian was cheerful.

"Do you have your first customer?"

"Yes!" replied Sebastian, raising his right fist clenching with success.

"How interesting." James slowly removed his golden glasses and polished them with a grey microfiber cloth. "Did you get paid?"

"Well, not yet."

"Then coffee is still on me," said James waiving to Inga. "One shot espresso and an iced Hibiscus tea, please."

"Would you like the espresso in an espresso cup?" Inga asked Sebastian.

"Yes, please. Would you have some lemon zest by any chance?"

"Of course we do."

"That will be fantastic. Thank you!"

"So," started James, "Tell me again about your first customer. If I remember correctly, last time we met you didn't even have a registered business. Am I right?"

"Well, you are correct James. But so much has happened in just a week"

Sebastian told James everything that had happened in the last few days. "Can you believe that the two of them don't know that they are organizing a trip for each other? This is going to be an amazing project!" ended Sebastian, drinking his espresso in one sip.

James nodded and looked straight into Sebastian's eyes "I hope you replied to the customers that you are not ready to take their request, yet. Didn't you?"

"Why would I do that? My note to them stated that my team would be working on their request and would send a proposal by the end of the week"

"Good. So you have time to say you are not ready."

"Actually... I have already sent them the itinerary this morning. Why would I tell them that I am not ready? Everything is pretty much in place and ready to go."

"Sebastian, you may have registered a company, but you are not ready for your first customer yet. You don't have a good infrastructure..." James drank some of his tea. As he was getting animated in his efforts to ground Sebastian, he felt his throat dry up like a stone in the full heat of the Sahara desert. "I'll rephrase it. You don't have ANY infrastructure. How are you going to handle this trip?"

"I have already made the reservations on my company name and paid with a credit card."

"Company?"

"Personal."

"Sebastian!" James slammed his hands on the table and rolled back his eyes. A few customers wondering if anything was wrong.

"I didn't have time to set up a company account, James. I'll do that first thing tomorrow morning."

"And what about the clothing? How are you going to buy them and ship them to destination?"

"All set. I found a small business in Wayzata that will take care of it."

"Your devices? The Travel ... something. Do they work?"

"Well... That is another story"

"Please, do tell me."

"They are not ready"

"And why should I be surprised?"

"My technical guy, Fernando is working around the clock to get them ready."

"You have a technical guy?"

"Oh yes, my neighbor is a genius. I'll bring him with me next time."

"Your entire core point of differentiation is being developed by your neighbor? Have you checked his background and his knowledge of patents and trademarks? Do you have any reference letter from previous customers? How in the world do you know he is qualified to do the job? No, please don't tell me. I don't think I can take any more for today. When is the departure?"

"Next weekend"

"I rest my case. Sebastian, are you insane?"

"The customers needed to leave as soon as possible and next week-end was the earliest I could find...."

"I did not mean you to find an earlier date. I meant to say you needed a LATER date!"

"I guess now would be quite late...."

"Yes it would, Sebastian. I do really hope you know what you are doing."

"Do most entrepreneurs?"

"What?"

"Know what they are doing?"

"No. And most of all, they do not listen."

"Well, I guess I am not doing that bad, am I?"

"Definitely not, Sebastian. Definitely not."

Sebastian left the meeting once again disappointed. But this time he had no time to think about it. Before getting into the car, he quickly dialed on his phone.

"Fernando, how are you?" Can I stop by for a minute? I need to get an update on the Travel Assistants."

"Sure Sebastian!" replied Fernando. "I'll have cold Antartica Brazilian beer ready for you."

"Great! I am on my way."

# CHAPTER XVI

*Shorewood, Minnesota*

Fernando Aguirre switched off his phone and went right back to work. All around him, a variety of automated gadgets executed household chores: spider-like lawn mowers, carefully tiptoeing around the yard to shape bushes, clip flowers, extrude unnecessary weeds and mow grass in various shapes and heights; flying droids policing the environment by searching for unwanted bugs while allowing all useful insects to visit, pollinate and color the yard; snake-shaped water dispenser bots going back and forward to gather and distribute just the right amount of water to each and every plant. Many other technologies invented by Fernando allowed him to take care of his pool and home without lifting a finger.

"This is the easiest and most fun assignment," he thought. A serving bot delivering a freshly squeezed lemonade which it filled with crushed ice and garnished with mint leaves.

"Would you like anything else to eat or drink?" the bot asked

"No, thank you. Do you mind calling my boss?"

"It will be my pleasure." The bot projected a tridimensional picture of a plane interior. A cacophony of lights and sensors filling most of the image.

"Are you flying again, boss?"

"Just another training session over the Ocean. You never know when you may need to know how to fly a plane."

"Boss, you own your own plane and you employee a team of pilots and flight attendants. Why would you need to know how to fly?" asked Fernando walking toward his emerald green swimming pool. A fish-like droid scanned the surface for bugs and leaves.

"You never know. I may need to escape from a dangerous situation or maybe the pilots won't be available when I need them… Or I may just decide to take a break and take a walk in the clouds by myself."

"Whatever, boss. You are always right." The pool water temperature, monitored by solar-powered sensors felt just right at the touch of his feet.

"How is it going with our new technology, Fernando?"

"We are almost done. I am running a few tests but the core functionalities are ready. The trip is going to be as smooth as it could be."

"Great job. I knew I could trust in you. Sorry for the fire drill. You are the only person I could trust with this assignment. And please, stop calling me boss. You make me feel like an old Mafia chief."

"And that would be a bad thing, right?"

"Definitely. By the way, Sebastian hates any word, reference, book, movie… Literally anything that could be even closely associated to the Godfather. Please avoid making any mention of it." A light blinked in the dashboard. "Need to go, Fernando. Landing time. You do not want me to end up in your pool… Although the water looks so inviting."

"My pool? Are you flying over me?" Asked Fernando screening the sky.

"Maybe… I never stay too far away from my investments. Bye Fernando."

"By Boss.. Ops Sorry… Whatever."


Fernando walked back to his chair still checking the horizon for flying objects.

"Mr. Fernando, Sebastian is walking through the front yard." Announced the bot concierge.

"Thank you. Time for everybody to take a siesta." All of a sudden, the magic garden full of electronics in motion felt silent and still.

He opened the front door to be confronted by two glass of sizzling white wine glasses.

"Verdicchio. Chilled at the right temperature. Just what we need for a nice, hot, Minnesotan afternoon." Smiled Sebastian.

"Thank you so much Sebastian. I was actually preparing a Brazilian beer testing for you but wine will work as well as we test a bit of your code. Come with me." Fernando took one of the glasses and started walking toward Sebastian's home. "Check your phone. You should have received a text message with an activation link. Click on it and your phone will start behaving like an Artificial Intelligence enhanced device."

"This is so exciting!" Sebastian drank his glass dry and activated his phone while trying to catch up with a fast walking Fernando.

"Welcome home Sebastian, how can I help you?"

"What's this? What's happening?" Sebastian asked Fernando, pointing to his phone.

"I setup a few beacons around the perimeter of your home. Try walking around. The beacons should activate as you walk and to and from different areas. However, I would..."

"Let's try!" said Sebastian cutting Fernando off. He turned around and walked back to his home.

"Sebastian, wait!" Warned him Fernando.

But Sebastian was too excited to listen and started roaming around his yard.

"Good afternoon Sebastian, this rose was planted 1 year ago. It was named after a royal princess and when it blooms, its color is a fantastic silver pink..."

Sebastian walked to a different place in his yard. "You are now walking through the Italian garden. So many varieties of herbs and vegetables were planted this year. I checked your refrigerator and I created a list of dishes you could prepare to take advantage of a fresh new crop. You would particularly enjoy..."

Sebastian moved forward. "Welcome to your swimming pool. The temperature outside is perfectly suitable for a swim."

Sebastian looked at Fernando, who had joined him in the backyard. "No Way!" Fernando started talking but Sebastian was on sensory overload. "Let's check what happens by getting closer to the garage door..."

"Welcome home, Sebastian. It is now time to activate the sprinkler system." Suddenly, small water diffusers came off the ground and the entire sprinkler system went off. Sebastian was drenched in a few seconds. He turned around to see Fernando laughing from a dry place in the yard. "I tried to tell you, but you did not listen!"

"This is amazing!" Sebastian, tried to clean up his sunglasses. "Is this your way of telling me that my Travel Concierge is ready?"

"Well… Yes and no." Replied Fernando, still laughing hard.

"What does that mean?"

"First of all, you don't have a physical device yet. You just have a phone app which works with your phone only, as I have modified its settings. The app is almost completed, but I need more time for review and test."

"How about a week?"

"For a new test? Sure. That should be plenty. I have a few scenarios that I would like to show you."

"No, I mean for deployment. My first customer departs a week from tomorrow."

"Are you insane?"

"Why is that everybody I talk to lately think the same thing of me lately? Let's put it another way. Can I have two devices ready by Wednesday? That way I shall still have time to ship them to the customer. Worst case scenario, I'll personally deliver them to their homes at night."

"Wednesday? For two devices? That is even less time than 1 week per device! You do realize I have a real job. Don't you?"

"Don't worry. I'll pay you."

"In what? Italian Ferrero chocolate? Illy Coffee?"

"Once my first trip is completed, I'll be able to pay you. What can you give me by Thursday evening?"

"Let me think." Fernando started walking back to his home. Head down clearly thinking about options. "I would hate to say no. Boss would not be happy… Plus this nuts Sebastian is such a fun guy…" He turned around and immediately regretted what came out of his mouth. "All right Sebastian, I think I can give you the Travel Concierge app working on one phone. The app will only have basic capabilities such as artificial intelligence, interactive capabilities and Search. It will mostly look like a regular phone with one app on it. The only difference is that the device will actually interact with your clients and learn from their searches. But you won't have the beacon component I just showed you."

"Fantastic! Now, really. Can you give me two devices? Please?"

"What part of "There is not enough time" you don't understand?"

"My family is Italian. Time is a foreign concept."

"Well, if your family is Italian you ARE in a foreign country!"

"Exactly. Time is something affecting you but not me."

"I am Brazilian."

"There you have it! A foreigner as well. And as Italians are 15% of Brazilian population, you may be part Italian as well. Welcome to the Timeless Zone!"

"You are insane."

"Again, your thought is in perfect alignment with 90% of the people I have been talking lately... Can I have two phones?"

"I'll try"

"Thank you!"

"Wait, it does not mean I'll be able to do it!"

"But you'll try!"

"Yes, I'll try. And you better have a nice Caribou card in my mailbox before next week is over."

"It's a deal!"

"By the way," Fernando turned back to Sebastian. "Can I use the other phone you gave me to set up the second Travel Assistant? Is that your phone as well?"

"Not exactly. It belongs to my best friend Gerard... Yes, use that number. I'll ask Gerard if I can borrow his phone for a couple of weeks."

"That will work. I'll send him the activation link. Please make sure he does NOT activate the Travel app until further notice."

"Don't worry. I'll take care of it as soon as he comes over tonight."

Fernando clicked on a few icons "Meanwhile, I am disactivating your appm for now. See you later, Sebastian."

"Thank you Fernando." Sebastian went back home and as he got nearby the garage door, the app popped up once again. This time he did not activate it. "I do not need to take a new shower. At least not outside."

# CHAPTER XVII

## *Shorewood, Minnesota*

Gerard was exhausted. He had tried to get to work early in the morning to take care of his key clients, leave early to finish packing, and move from his apartment in downtown Minneapolis to Sebastian's home. But all of his planning had come to a halt when Vanessa Von Struttenberger, VP of Sales, had called him in her office for a "quick" checkpoint. By the time all of her questions had been answered in a satisfactory manner, Gerard's email box and voicemails were once again out of control. At 7:00 p.m., Gerard raised his white flag. "Time to get back home and finish packing. Everything else can wait until tomorrow morning." He stopped by his old apartment to gather as many clothes and essentials he could fit in his car and drove South-West to his new living space in Chanhassen.

He turned into the subdivision that would become his new neighborhood. Luscious plants decorated the entrance to his new community. Manicured sidewalks guided the drivers through winding streets. Fountains with colorful lights decorated ponds and lakes. Green, spotless parks dotted the area. "It will be a nice transition to a better lifestyle", he thought. "If only work would allow me to take a walk every once in a while."

As he approached Sebastian's home, Gerard realized that he did not have a remote garage opener. "I must have left it in the house last time I was at Sebastian's. I was so upset by the fact that he tricked me in joining his crazy venture." He parked the car just opposite the house and started walking toward the front door.

"Welcome home Gerard!"

"What the…"

"Sebastian is waiting for you inside. Dinner is ready and the wine is chilled. To enable all features of this Travel Concierge, please activate the app."

"What app!" Said Gerard getting closer to the door.

"Please click on the orange button to activate the app"

"George clicked on the button and…"

"Son of a…"

The sprinkler system turned on showering Gerard with cold water. Outdoor lights went on lighting up the house like a Christmas tree ready for the holidays and the garage door opened.

"Benvenuto a casa!"[8] Said Sebastian opening the door and popping a bottle of Spumante. He looked at a drenched, surprised and grumpy Gerard.

"I guess you activated the Travel Concierge app. How did you like it?"

"Seriously?" Droplets of water streamed down his short, black hair.

"Well, It's not perfect but your friend Fernando will have it completed in a few days. You and I are the only two lucky people in the entire WOLRD to be able to test it!"

"You are crazy! I am soaked! And who in the Hell is Fernando?"

"Why? Fernando! The guy you referred me to."

"I didn't refer you to this Fernando guy. I referred you to Dr. Kowalski!"

"The shrink?"

"Yes, Sebastian. The Shrink!"

Sebastian drank the remaining of his spumante. "Oh. That explains… Well, details, details. Now, bring in your car and please take off your shoes. You are all wet. The cleaning crew came today and the house is spotless. Let's try to keep it clean, shall we?" And with that, Sebastian went back inside without offering to help or at least providing Gerard a towel.

---

8  Welcome Home!

# CHAPTER XVIII

## Santa Maria La Scala, Sicily

"Mum! Dad! Today I went on an excursion. I was with a class of children of my age. We followed a very old street carved in the rocks and we walked downhill to the sea. The beach was full of rocks. I could not find any spot with sand to build a castle. But I found a small waterfall coming from the rocky cliff. The water was so fresh and delicious!" Good night mum and dad. Good night brother and sister."

# PART IV

*Sebastian hopes for some more, a "mouse" gets lost in a church and Laura gets loose.*
*Meanwhile, Gerard surrenders... his phone... or does he?*

# CHAPTER XIX

## *Shorewood, Minnesota*

Sebastian spent the rest of the weekend checking details of the trip to Italy, connecting with Robbie to make sure all the clothes would be ready on time, and testing the Travel Concierge app. But there was one key task that still had to be completed. Well…two.

Gerard had just finished unpacking his belongings in his new room. It was a spacious bedroom with a large closet and plenty of space for a sofa near a window overlooking the garden downstairs; perfect for relaxing evening readings. He had also managed to fit a desk, and some bookshelves which he filled with some Finance and Business books, and a few biographies of successful CEOs and politicians. He sat on his sofa to enjoy a cold beer from the local Excelsior brewery.

Sebastian stopped by the bedroom door and leaned against the door frame: one arm folded on his chest, the other playing with a martini. "How is it going, Gerard. Did you unpack everything?"

"Yes, I think I am pretty done." Gerard took a sip of fresh, blond beer. "Thank you Sebastian. This room is perfect."

"Great! I am glad you like it," replied Sebastian taking a sip of his drink. "I just have a quick, silly question."

"Sure. Shoot"

"You have a work phone, right?"

"You mean a phone that I can use for work purposes?" Gerard set his beer on his grandmother antique side table, a leather coaster protecting the delicate suffice.

"Yes. A phone you use to make and receive calls for work and you can also call in case of emergency. You have one, right?"

"What are you talking about? What kind of emergency?" Gerard stood up and got closer to Sebastian. "Something is up. I better pay attention," he thought.

"I don't know, Gerard, I may be in a foreign country and I may suddenly need help… What if you are not able to answer your personal phone… I am just thinking about hypothetical scenarios… Something like that."

"No need to think about that, Sebastian. I always have both my phones. And you are not in danger in a foreign country."

"Well…" Sebastian sat on Gerard's chair and drank down Gerard's bottle of beer in one, long sip.

"Oh no. What did you do now?" Gerard took the bottle away from Sebastian's hands, knowing very well that his grandmother's table would have not been spared a permanent stain.

"The thing is, Gerard… As you know, I have two clients leaving at the same time for Italy."

"And?"

"I only have one prototype phone."

"And?" Gerard threw away the bottle into a recycling trash container he had set up in his bathroom.

"I need two Travel Concierge devices. Well, as I only have the app, at the moment, I just need two phones set with the appropriate settings so that the app would work.

"Can't you just buy another phone?"

"I could, but Fernando would not be able to program it on time. Yours is already programmed and tested…"

"You mean hacked?"

"Well, I wouldn't be so negative… What if…" Sebastian stood up and got closer to Gerard.

"No!"

"I have not asked anything yet"

"No!"

"Could I 'borrow' your phone for a week?"

"No way, Sebastian!" Gerard started walking toward the door. Then he realized that the room was actually his own room. He turned around and gestured Sebastian to leave.

Sebastian started walking toward the door. "Ok, I understand. But seriously, what could go wrong? I'll give it back to you after the trip. Don't worry. Fernando will make a full backup before I give it to the clients."

"No"

"You will not even notice. You barely use it at all!"

"No"

"I could pay you for the rental ..."

"No"

"Anything I could give you in exchange?"

"No"

"All right. I'll figure out something." He slowly paced up and down the room seriously testing Gerard's patience. "I guess I'll have to find a solution for our company..."

"You mean *YOUR*?" Gerard pointed toward Sebastian

"No... *OUR*." Sebastian pointed to both of them with his hands "Your name ... and your signature are on the Company's documents." He motioned Gerard to forget about everything and started walking away.

"Wait! What are you planning to do?"

"At the end of the day, our clients don't even know that the devices are part of the overall experience." Sebastian started playing with his hair as he usually did when he was nervous.

"Is there any mention of it on the website?"

"Well, on the website... yes. But in our proposal to the clients there is no mention that the Travel Concierge devices would be provided"

"You mean *YOUR* proposal." Stressed Gerard.

"*OUR* proposal." Sebastian sighted. "You signed it as well..."

"What!?"

"I have your signature on... file. The Company's name is Gerard and

81

Sebastian! I needed a signature from Gerard too."

"Sebastian, you are crazy!"

"I know, you tell me all the time. "

"Just to remind that to you. In case you forget."

"Thank you. You are very kind." He paused, then started "So?"

"What?"

"Can I borrow your phone?"

"NO!"

Sebastian left the room. "There is still time to make him change his mind." He thought walking down the stairs. As he approached the front door, he looked at a painting hanging on the right side of the entrance. It was nothing special. Just a rocky beach scene from Sicily.

*When was the last time I was in Sicily?*

Sebastian could not remember a specific date. Just the feeling of the sun on his skin on that last summer by the Mediterranean Sea: the water was so crystal and green, you could see fish and crabs moving underneath the surface.

On the painting, he lightly traced with his fingers the length of the beach. On the right side of the shore, far in the distance, there was a very large rock standing tall above the sea.

*I remember a similar rock by the sea. My cousins and I used to call it "the castle"*

He closed his eyes and tried to recall childhood scenes of competition among cousins to conquer the castle and become the prince of it for a day. At the end of the fight they would just lie on top of the rock to recover and relax. How magnificent was the feeling of sunbathing while towering over the sea on that perfect sculpture of Mother Nature.

"it's time for me to go back." He wondered if he would have had time to stop by the rocky beach and visit his castle by the sea once more.

# CHAPTER XX

*Acireale, Sicily*

"Mum! Dad! I went back to the beach. This time all by myself. I found a gigantic rock as big as a royal castle. When I got on top of it, I imaged myself to be a king and from my tall throne, I looked out to the sea. I could see hundreds of sailing boats dotting the water. I imagined that maybe, one day, you would all be on one of those boats... Well, lights are off. Time to go to bed. Good night mum and dad. Good night little brother and big sister"

# CHAPTER XXI

*Acireale, Sicily*

T he talented woodworkers had been fast. A new glass door provided once more some refuge to Don Calogero as parishioners filled the Cathedral at all times of the day either to pray or just enjoy a cool retreat from the hot Sicilian Summer heat. Gone were the elaborately chiseled wooden glyphs and the colorful stained glass. Gone were St. Michael and the evil dragon. The new door was simpler and lighter: its glass clear and plain.

Don Calogero missed his daily interactions with a wicked mythological creature that never existed at all except in the minds of simple people. His problems were concrete and the impact could dramatically affect a young life. A shiny, holy sword would not be enough. His problems required more pragmatic solutions and time was not on his side.

"Have they left, Donna Carmela?"

"Yes." She replied, closing the door behind her and sitting by Don Calogero's desk. "All went well. They checked every room in the building and each and every shrub in the children's outdoor play area. They even entered inside the confessionary. But still… They did not find anything out of the ordinary." Her wooden rosary clutched by her trembling hands.

"Were they supposed to?" Don Calogero opened his Bible looking randomly for a quote.

"Somebody at the market told them that a refugee child was hiding inside

84

the walls of this sacred place. Those sbirri[9] listened to the rumors and immediately came over to St. Michael to check if anybody was hiding inside the church.

"Donna Carmela, we need to be honest," Don Calogero continued looking at the Bible pretending to mentally read a passage with his right pointer finger. "We never talked about hosting a refugee child INSIDE the church, have we?"

"No, Don Calogero, we never did."

"Otherwise, Donna Carmela, I would be in really bad troubles by having declared a false statement to the policemen."

"Yes, Don Calogero."

"Have you said anything to them, Donna Carmela?"

"Of course not, Don Calogero. I always follow my late husband's motto. God save his soul."

"Which is?"

"Listen a lot. Talk just a little."

"Good to know, Donna Carmela. Good to know. Please let me know if they come back. Now I need to focus on our afternoon sermon."

Donna Carmela stood up and started walking out of the Sacristy.

"Donna Carmela. Just for curiosity…"

"Yes, Don Calogero." She stopped by the glass door. Hand on the door handle.

"Did you show them the Bell Tower?"

"Of course I did. I showed them the entrance and they started going upstairs… But it was too dark and they soon came out of it."

"Good. Good. I hear there is a little *MOUSE*. We don't want to give them the wrong impression…"

"Of course, Don Calogero. I'll leave you to your readings then. See you at Mass." She opened the door and started walking into the main nave of the Church: the most beautiful and peaceful place she had ever known.

"Donna Carmela! One last thing."

---

[9] Depreciative for policemen

She turned around and went back into the sacristy. Don Calogero still searching for some inspirational Bible verse.

"Yes, Don Calogero."

"You said the staircase inside the Bell Tower was dark. Is the light system not working again?"

A smile appeared on Donna Carmela "I don't recall you and I talking about the light system being fixed. Have we? Otherwise, I would be in big troubles for having declared false to the authorities..."

Don Calogero lifted his eyes from the Bible, looked up to Donna Carmela's concerned eyes and smiled..."You are correct, Donna Carmela, we never did... I'll see you at Mass then."

Relieved, Donna Carmela closed the door behind her.

Don Calogero stood up from his chair and walked toward his wardrobe. He opened the heavy cherry wood doors and went through his many white tunics searching for the perfect attire to wear during the afternoon Mass.

"There it is!"

He got himself ready and stopped by a mirror. "As always, Donna Carmela has done a great job."

He lifted his stole and positioned it on top of his tunic. He looked at himself in the mirror and, satisfied, traced the white garment with his fingers down to a small area where a faded coffee stain lingered almost undetectable. He then walked to his desk to pick up his Bible. The Leather cover of it had been designed a few years earlier by one of his parishioners and resembled the design of the old stained glass door -St. Michael still stood fierce to protect humanity against a dragon. A recent addition made the beast a little bit more defiant: two ruby red pieces of glass looked up straight to Don Calogero.

"Yes, I know. Even the best of us host a little bit of evil inside. That is what makes us human." He smiled to the dragon and walked toward the altar. "Now, let's repent our sins."

# CHAPTER XXII

*Chanhassen, Minnesota*

Devices packed into two cobalt blue boxes wrapped in a golden ribbon and safely secured on the passenger seat, Sebastian entered the address of his customers on his car's GPS system. "135 Nestled Woods, Chanhassen. It can't be that far away," he thought.

He drove through a neighborhood still in construction. Its lands, waters and wild life, once owned by a world-renowned singer had been spared by urban development until his death. Gone were the rolling, Tuscan-like hills that had once adorned Route 5 with shades of emerald greens in spring and auburn reds and yellows in fall. Spruce Way, Springdale Ln, Fawn Hill Ct and a few more street names, were everything left.

Sebastian turned right on Springdale Trail and drove all the way down to the end of the street, where four homes with spotless front yards welcomed children in the most coveted cul-de-sac of the neighborhood.

"Turn left on Nestled Woods. Destination is on your right" announced his navigation system.

Although still technically part of the same street, Springdale Trail, for some reason the builder had decided that three lucky homes, sharing the same driveway should be called Nestled Woods instead. And so hidden those homes where by the sharp curve of its driveway and the thick vegetation, that Sebastian had almost missed them.

He was now sitting inside his car, parked just at the entrance of Nestled Woods, trying to decide what to do. "I could just walk up and hope that only one of the two would be at home to find his or her device waiting... But how can I make sure that the right device goes to the right person? If I give the device and the travel plans to the wrong person, I will ruin the surprise and that would make it for a very angry first customer! Well, in this case two."

To make the situation worse, the couple lived at the very end of the street. "There is no way I could leave the devices at the front door and remain undetected. They would see me before I could get back to the car."

Sebastian looked at the two envelopes he had filled out with travel arrangements. One letter was addressed to John. One to his wife Laura. "I wonder if there is anything I can do to take at least one of the two out of the house?" Suddenly an idea hit him. John had found his business card at the coffee shop in Excelsior. "Maybe he was there to buy something special... Let's try."

* * *

*"Dear John, all information related to your trip, scheduled for Friday afternoon, 4:45 pm, has been mailed to your home address. Included in your travel package, you will find our proprietary invention, Mobile Travel Concierge (MTC). Your MTC will guide you through your journey and will provide you immediate assistance for anything you may need while overseas. Once your trip has been completed please use the box you will receive to mail the MTC back to us.*

*In addition, your personalized collection of clothes and accessories has been already shipped to your receiving destination. You will find everything you need inside the room we have selected for you at Pensione Mirabella in Aquilia Beach, Sicily. Please remember to activate your MTC on the day of your departure.*

*Kind Regards,*
  *Gerard and Sebastian*

*P.S. Your transfer to the airport has been scheduled for 12:30 p.m. Our driver will pick you up at your front door. We have taken care of everything but you may want to bring with you something that will make the journey to the airport –and the surprise- very special. Some of our clients enjoy chocolate, pastries and other personal way of connecting with their significant other.*

John was so excited, he did not think about it twice. He ran to the car and started driving to Inga's Café in Excelsior. On the way out of his driveway, he noticed a car at the end of the cul-de-sac, just by the mailboxes.

\* \* \*

As soon as the red Jeep drove out of sight, Sebastian left his car and started walking toward Nestled Woods Ln keeping a steady step: not too slow –he did not have much time- but not too fast to not alert anybody who may notice him walking up the street. He got to the front door and left the package for Laura. He then rang the doorbell and quickly moved away.

"I made it!" Sebastian exclaimed once safe inside the car. "Laura will open the door and get her package while John will get his package in the mailbox as soon as he will get back home."

He started the engine but then stopped it again. "What if Laura is not at home? What if John gets back home before Laura and finds her device instead? I have to be sure. I can't mess this up."

He left the car and walked back to the house. It was starting to get dark so indoor lights were visible all over the street but... But not in John's house. He had made a mistake. Laura had not come back from work and John had been the only one at home. "Darn! What do I do now?"

Sebastian quickly sent a text to Laura to let her know that her travel documentation had been delivered at her front door, then walked back to his car. A black Nissan drove by and he instinctively waved.

"Was that Laura? Or maybe a neighbor?" He did not have much time. Once back to the car, he put the second envelope in the mailbox, then he sent a text to John to let him know that his travel arrangements had been delivered to his mailbox. He finally drove the car a little bit up the street to monitor the mailboxes. He was hoping John would see his message and check the mail before getting back home.

\* \* \*

"For Heaven sake. Why would anybody park nearby the mailboxes?" Laura thought. Upset for not being able to get the mail on her way home, Laura parked her car in the garage and got into the house. John was not at home. "Strange. Usually he would be home making dinner by this time." She picked up her mobile phone to send him a message when she noticed new email from the travel agency.

*"Your travel plans have been delivered to the front door."* Without wasting any time, Laura run to the door. "The last thing I need is John to find out!". There it was. A blue and gold package from *Gerard and Sebastian Travels, what is your dream?*

*"Handle with care",* the label said. And so she did.

\* \* \*

John had just made his purchase of chocolate croissant, Laura's preferred, when his phone buzzed. A message sent from the travel agency announced that a package had been delivered. "The mailbox! Laura always gets the mail before getting home." He quickly paid his bill and rushed to his car.

John ran through a couple of lights "Was that a dark yellow? Maybe a red?" before finally getting into his subdivision. He reached the cul-de-sac, parked by the mailbox, and quickly slid to the passenger's seat. He had just rolled down the window to open the mailbox when he heard a familiar voice.

"John! "

Heart beating fast, without turning around, he opened the mailbox and got hold of a blue and gold package. "It has to be the one!" He threw the package in the car through the side window.

Laura approached by the mailbox. "I was worried. You are usually home before me. Everything ok?"

"Oh yes," he said picking up the remaining mail.

"I could not get the mail earlier on. Some stupid neighbor had parked his car nearby the mailbox and I could not open the box. Hand it to me. I'll take care of it. You know how much I enjoy it."

"Of course", said John, handing over the mail like a child busted eating cookies from the forbidden cookie jar. "At least the travel agency's package is in the car." He thought, gently kicking the blue and gold box under the car seat. "Jump in the car, I'll drive you home." He volunteered trying to figure out a way to hide his surprise.

"Nonsense! Such a great afternoon in Minnesota. I'll take a walk. See you at home."

"That was close!" he thought.

# CHAPTER XXIII

*Acireale, Sicily*

"Mum! Dad! I feel so much better. My teacher said I had a sunstroke. I must have had too much sun when I went to the beach a couple of days ago. I felt so sick. But now I am better. My teacher and my headmaster take a good care of me. Good night mum and dad. God night big sister. Good night little brother."

# PART V

*A forgotten family gets involved, a couple gets a new start, Sebastian gets on a plane and a boy gets in trouble. Meanwhile, Gerard doesn't get it.*

# CHAPTER XXIV

*Acireale, Sicily*

"He is coming! I just saw his reservation."

"I know. His father sent me a message."

"Does he know?"

"I don't think so."

"They used to come over so frequently when he was a little boy... I remember us playing on the beach for hours. What happened?"

"His father and I had an argument."

"About what?"

"Something I kept hidden."

"You lied to him?"

"After all I did to him? How could I? I just never told him the full truth... Until..."

"What did you tell him?"

"It was a horrible day. Sebastian's mother had just died giving birth to his sister and his dad was inconsolable. The doctors had prescribed him some strong prescription to keep him sedated. I was walking up and down this balcony singing a lullaby to the little girl... She was so beautiful."

"Where was Sebastian?"

"You, Sebastian and the other kids were all playing by the beach, as usual: clueless of the tragedy that had just hit us. I thought his father was sleeping and I didn't realize he was listening. I said something horrible at a time when he was most vulnerable."

"Mamma, what did you say?"

"I was talking to myself. My heart was broken as well. I said "I wish you could see how beautiful your grandchildren are. I wish you were here with me to help me to console your child. If only you knew he was ever born, I could call you and ask you for help."

"You never told him his father was alive?"

"How could I? It was better for him to think that his father had died when he was still an infant, than to know that somewhere out there, there is a man who has no idea he was ever born."

"Mamma![10]"

"When I turned around, he was staring at me with his big, red eyes. He didn't say anything. He took the little girl from me and called Sebastian. He left town and did not return my calls for a long time. Until he finally called me."

"Why?"

"He asked me about his father and begged me to tell him his name."

"Did you?"

"Yes. I did. It was the least I could do. Also… He promised me I would get pictures and updates of the little ones every now and then."

"Is that the reason why he went to the United States?"

"Yes."

"You said that he sent you a message to let you know Sebastian was on his way to Sicily. Why?"

"He needs help. I am Sebastian's grandmother. I would do anything for him… And you would as well."

"Me? Why am I involved in this now?"

"Because you are his aunt. We are his family. And this is what families do. We help each other."

---

[10] Mother

# CHAPTER XXV

*Chanhassen, Minnesota*

I t was a sunny morning when John made Laura's favorite breakfast: freshly baked biscuits, bacon, scrambled eggs, Greek yogurt sprinkled with honey, grape juice, coffee, and to top it off, Inga's Café' Excelsior's chocolate croissants. He added a nice rose just picked from their Italian garden.

John set up everything on large tray and started walking upstairs to their bedroom. He was half a way up, when he heard the garage door opening. He turned around and walked back downstairs. An exceptionally serene Laura came out of the garage door carrying two Kowalski paper bags in her hands. They both looked at each other and started laughing.

"I guess there is no way I can surprise you!" said Laura.

"Well, I guess I could say the same." replied John. "Would you like to have some breakfast before going to work? Such a glorious day, today."

"Yes, said Laura. It is a nice day. I got you Kowalski's Italian pastries. Fresh and yummy."

"And I made your favorite breakfast... Well, maybe we could call it a brunch."

They both laughed and looked at each other. And talked. Like they had not done in a long time.

"I was wondering", started John... scratching his full head of hair.

"Oh oh..., you sound and look dangerously serious now. Should I be worried?" Laura crossed her hands.

"No, No. I was wondering. We never take time off from work. What would you think if we take a few days? Maybe a week?"

"Oh, is that the reason why you made that breakfast for me?"

"Well, I must admit... Yes."

"I'll tell you what. I too was wondering..."

"Do tell," said John getting closer and closer to Laura.

"I think we could take a couple of days off."

"What about starting today?" John took the rose out of the vase and offered it to Laura.

"I think work could survive without me. Let me make a couple of calls." She picked up her phone and started dialing, then suddenly stopped "With that said, what you would like to do today?"

"Well," said John. "First of all, I would like to have a long breakfast."

"And then?"

"I think we could start where we were this morning."

"Excuse me?" said Laura, puzzled.

"In bed." John winked, offered a hand to Laura, and walked her upstairs.

# CHAPTER XXVI

*Shorewood, Minnesota*

"All right Gerard, I think I have everything I need. Are you sure you will be ok?" Sebastian panted, carrying his luggage downstairs.

"I'll survive," replied Gerard from the kitchen. He moved to the next page of his morning newspaper while sipping a cup of coffee. "I still don't understand why you need to fly to Italy with your customers."

Sebastian left his luggage and backpack near the front door and walked into the kitchen, "You mean OUR customers? I have to! This is our first trip. These are our first customers. We need to make sure everything goes according to plan. Besides, I am still not confident the Travel Concierges will work properly... So I asked Fernando to set up a full monitoring system on my PC. This way, I can check what is going on at any time."

Gerard put down his newspaper "Wait. Are you saying that you are going to spy on the clients? I thought you were just going to check hotels and service providers of all the activities you have planned. I didn't realize you were going all Sherlock Holmes on me!"

"You have read too many mystery books." Sebastian checked his wallet to make sure he had credit cards and passport. "I am only going to check on them every once in a while. By the way, do you remember the garage code?"

"I have it saved on my phone." Gerard went back to read his newspaper.

"Front door key?"

"Three copies. One in the car, one on my dresser, one in my work bag."

"Phone number?" Sebastian walked to the front door to check if the taxi

99

driver had arrived.

"I already have it memorized in my contact list."

"No, I meant my new one."

"You have a new phone?" exclaimed Gerard, folding his newspaper as he expected a long explanation coming his way. "You bought a new phone? You. The cheapest person I know."

Sebastian went back to the kitchen as the taxi driver had not arrived yet. "Frugal. I am frugal. I am not cheap. I just bought a basic smart phone."

"Why? You already have one."

"I had to use my phone for our customers. Fernando was able to re-program my phone and setup a special app so that it now functions as a full Travel Concierge device."

"Are you joking?" George walked toward his naïve friend. "What if the clients won't give you the phone back?" He gently knocked on Sebastian's head "Anybody in there?"

Sebastian breathed in Gerard's cologne. *He is so close I could kiss him!* "Of course they will," he replied. "I trust them."

"You have never met them!"

*How I love it when he becomes all puffy red.* "I trust they will do the right thing."

"Why, Sebastian? Why would they"

"Because that is what I would do. Besides, I have their credit card information. I can always charge them for the new phone."

"Good point," exhaled Gerard. "For once, you are saying something that makes sense." Gerard went back to the kitchen table. Newspaper back open. "All right, see you next week, then. Please do not mess everything up and come back all in one piece."

"You sound like my mother." The doorbell ring announced the arrival of a taxi driver.

"No Sebastian. I sound like the other 50% of a company shareholder."

"Now YOU make sense, partner!" Sebastian got closer to Gerard and opened his arms. "Can I get a bye-bye hug?"

"Whatever." Gerard hugged his friend and gave him a pat on his head.

"Come back in one piece, ok?"

Sebastian nodded.

"Good. Get out of my sight and try not to get us in a lawsuit."

"I won't. Ciao." *God, I could kiss you right now!*

Sebastian left Gerard in the kitchen got into his taxi. He looked outside the window, his neighbors' homes passing by one after the other. He loved when trips began. It was a time of fullness: the expectation of a great time; the thrill of the unexpected; the uncertainty of the trip itself. "Always prepare for the worst case scenario." Maarten had told him.

"Destination?" said the taxi driver.

"Minneapolis-St. Paul airport. May the adventure begin!"

# CHAPTER XXVII

## *Chanhassen, Minnesota*

"Laura, are you ready? Our taxi is outside waiting. I have organized a little surprise for us." John had packed all electronics, passports, a couple of books and a few essentials in his backpack. All fit nicely. He did not want Laura to think that they were going on a trip. And overseas!

"I am coming, John!" Replied Laura. "Where in the world are the passports?" Looking frantically in every possible drawer, Laura had put everything she needed for the trip and a few items for John in a backpack. The only things missing were electronics and passports. "All right. Who care about the electronics?" she thought. "But we need the passports. He must know where they are."

"John?"

"Yes, honey."

"There is one thing I want to make sure we take care of while we are on vacation."

"Sure. Tell me."

"Can you remind me where the passports are? I want to make sure we renew them. Who knows? We may decide to take a trip at some point and right now I heard on the news that it takes about 3-6 months to get them renewed."

"Do not worry. I already thought about it. They will last for a very long time. I always have them with me in my travel bag. Just in case we need two different IDs. Let's go honey, the taxi driver won't wait for long."

"Here I am. Ready for a great adventure!" She smiled. *Just wait until I ask him for the passports as I need them to go to Italy!*

Laura and John locked the house and got into the taxi. They looked at their home like if it was the first time. It had so many fantastic memories. But at the same time, it reminded them of Lilly.

"We should start thinking about moving somewhere else," thought John. "Maybe I can convince Laura during the trip."

"This home has been great for us but it may be time to move on. Maybe I will convince him to put the house on the market during the trip," thought Laura.

"Destination?" Asked the taxi driver.

"Inga's Café' in Excelsior, replied John. "We'll grab some coffee and then I'll let you know where our next stop will be. Thank you."

"Sure sir."

The taxi driver left Nestled Woods Lane. Both John and Laura could not wait to surprise each other. What did the note say? "At exactly 12:31 p.m., your Travel Concierge will automatically activate."

"Inga's Café' Excelsior was as usual jammed with people trying to enjoy every single minute of Minnesota's short summer. Bikers in full gear were talking about their latest achievements. Mothers were getting a short break while the children were at camp. Retirees, back from Florida or many other Southern locations, were reconnecting with friends after a long winter season.

Laura and John purchased their lunch snacks. "Please pick us up in 30 minutes," they had told the driver. They had been able to secure their preferred seat at the extreme south corner of the Cafe'. The one that had the best view of Lake Minnetonka.

"You know John, I was thinking..."

"I think I know what you are thinking."

"Really? Surprise me."

"I think we are due for something out of ordinary."

"Well, well, Mr. John. You really are a man full of surprises. What have you got in your mind? I thought we had already explored your universe of options this morning…"

"Not completely. I have a few cards still to play."

"And since when did you become a gambler?"

"Just a few weeks ago. And right now I have a lot at stake."

"You are now both scaring me and intriguing me."

"Here is the thing. Our last couple of years have been very intense. Our hearts will always have room for Lilly and she will never leave us. But…"

"But?"

"It's you and me now. And we are still together, right?"

"Yes."

"So…"

"Before you say anything, I have a surprise for you, John. Let me show you something." Laura started opening her purse.

"Yes, I also have something to show you." John started opening his backpack.

"Good afternoon John, your Travel Concierge has been activated. Whatever your dream is, it has just began"

"Good afternoon Laura, I am Michele, your Travel Concierge. Whatever your dream is, it has just begun."

John and Laura looked at each other.

"You…"said Laura.

"Michele? I have not been able to get through the full setup. Mine does not even have a name… You have organized something with my same agency! Where?"

"Well, my gambler. Where are we going?" smiled Laura

"ITALY!" John and Laura both screamed and jumped. They held each other and kissed like two teenagers.

"I just love my little place," Inga thought looking at them.

"Please tell me you have the passports" said Laura.

"Yes." Said John "and the electronics as well."

"You devil! I have been looking for those stupid things all night!"

"Well, let's get to the airport. Plenty of time to catch up with sleep on the plane."

# CHAPTER XXVII

Just then, the taxi driver arrived. Laura and John held each other all the way to the airport. No words were necessary. Just the touch of each other hands.

# CHAPTER XXVIII

*Acireale, Sicily*

"Mum! Dad! Today I played a new game. While we were hiding in the fish market, some of the children talked to a couple of older men in uniform. I think the men liked the game a lot. In fact, they started looking for me and the other kids. But we were fast and hid very well. One of the men almost found me but I quickly hid myself in a big box full of vegetables. I don't think they were good ones as they smelled a bit … But the trick worked. When I went back to school, my teacher looked at me from head to toe and put her fists on her hips. She was not happy at all!

She gestured with her right hand to say "No! No!" and sent me to the bathroom to wash myself with a lot of soap. She also gave me new clothes and threw away the old ones. Now I smell like lemons and I feel very clean. But I feel a bit tired. I think I'll take a nap. Good night mum and dad. Good night brother and sister."

# CHAPTER XXIX

### *Minneapolis-St. Paul Airport, Minnesota*

"Welcome to Minneapolis-St. Paul Airport, your taxi fare has been already paid and your luggage to Italy has been checked. Please follow me to the closest CLEAR station for your security screening."

"John, did you?"

"Yes, Laura, I got the same message. This is quite a different experience, isn't it?"

"Yes, indeed! I wonder what clothes you have chosen for me."

Well, the good news is that we are going to have two sets. The one I ordered and the ones you did." Smiled John.

John and Laura crossed the glass doors of the airport. Once inside, they walked toward unknown paths, leaving their past behind: glass doors closing after them like a protective shield.

\* \* \*

"Perfectly on time. Three hours before schedule." Though Sebastian looking outside the window of his taxi to admire the sprawling Minneapolis/St. Paul airport. "Plenty of time to upload my apps on the iPad, get the latest Concierge upgrade for my phone, and review my travel schedule."

"How much do I owe you?" Sebastian asked the taxi driver.

"It will be eighty-five dollars. Thank you"

"Here is my Amex. Can you charge $100 to include tip?"

"Certainly, sir".

The taxi driver scanned Sebastian credit card and waited for the transaction to be completed.

"I can't wait to be back to Italy. Once my clients will be back home, I'll be able to spend a full extra day shopping or sightseeing. So many things on my wish list!"

"Sir, I am having some trouble with your credit card." the taxi driver woke him up from his Italian dream. "Would you have another card I could try instead?" He turned toward Sebastian and gave him back his card.

"Sure... Can you try once again? Maybe a connection issue?"

"I have already tried a few times. It really does not go through. You may want to call your bank before flying... Just in case"

"Here is my $100 cash." He sadly parted from a good portion of his duty-free slush fund.

"Thank you sir."

"You are welcome." Sebastian mentally cancelled his planned stop by the Duty Free on his way back to the United States and got out of the taxi. "I better call the bank. I need my card to work or I'll be in big trouble..."

The taxi driver gave him his luggage. "Here you are sir."

"Thank you. Have a great day." Sebastian said. Still thinking about millions of reasons why his card would not work. He switched on his phone and looked for the phone number of Gloria McDonald, his financial advisor.

"Darn! I forgot this is my new phone. All of my contacts are saved on my other phone. The one now used by John. I should have transferred my contacts to the new phone before giving the other one away." He pondered a few options. "No reason to panic. Let's get through check-in and security. I can call Gloria from the gate."

Once inside the airport, Sebastian walked to the closest self-service check-in machine. He scanned his credit card to retrieve his reservation but the machine did not collaborate. "May I help you sir?" A smiling check-in officer approached.

"That would be wonderful! Thank you." Sebastian said, scratching his head. "My credit card is not working. Is there any other way to print out my ticket?"

"Of course, there is. Let me help you." The check-in officer took control of the machine. "Would you have your ID or passport with you? It will work as well... Unless you are flying international, of course."

"Ugh! I guess that's the problem," replied Sebastian. "I am actually going to Italy."

"In that case, sir, I am really sorry but you will have to go through the regular line at the International Transfers desk."

Sebastian thanked the check-in officer started walking toward a very crowded line of people and suitcases. "Thank God I have plenty of time! This line is going to take forever." Sebastian looked around. So many lives and stories. New beginnings, broken hearts, expectations for upcoming family vacations, worry over sick family members.

The line slowly moved forward in twists and turns: travelers matched with their own personal journey progressing toward the next step. "May I have your passport sir?"

"Excuse me?"

"Your passport, sir. I need it to check your reservation." The soft, but assertive, voice of the ticket agent woke him up from his state of day dreaming.

"Of course, of course." Sebastian picked up his passport from the backpack. One of Fernando's last minute gift, the backpack also functioned as a portable solar power charger and offered many functional hidden pockets for the storage of Sebastian's large collection of gadgets. "Here it is madam."

Sebastian positioned his luggage on the scale emptying his lungs of air, as if making himself smaller and lighter would affect the weight of his luggage. He closed his eyes and after a couple of prayers to his ancestral Sicilian/Greek Gods, he opened up to find out that his luggage had barely made it to the maximum weight allowed. "Phew! At least I saved some money." He thought.

The clinking sound of perfectly manicured hands rhythmically marked the passing of time needed to process the booking. "Very well, Mr. Sebastian.

All looks good." She smiled and looked at Sebastian. "It will be $50."

"Excuse me?"

"For your luggage. The luggage fee is $50."

"But I am a club member. Isn't the luggage included?"

"Only if you check-in with your credit card. Do you have your credit card?"

"Yes, but it looks like it is not working. Could you use it anyway?"

"I am sorry. I need a valid credit card to be able to waive the fee"

"Here is my checking card. How much did you say is the fee?"

"$50"

"Gosh! All right." Sebastian opened his wallet and removed another portion of his slush funds "I still have some money left."

Sebastian mentally made a quick calculation of how much he had already deducted from his already meager new business owner funds. And he had not even left the airport yet.

"I guess I have no choice." He reluctantly separated from his hard-earned small treasure.

"Thank you for flying with us. Please follow directions to the closest security check. And be fast. Your flight to JFK will depart soon."

"Soon?" Sebastian finally realized how much time he had spent getting through the ticketing phase. And he still had the security check to go through. He rushed to the closest line hoping for the best.

# CHAPTER XXX

## *Minneapolis-St. Paul Airport, Minnesota*

"John, based upon your profile, I took the liberty to pre-purchase some pastries for you and Laura. They are ready for pick up at *Il Forno*[11], nearby Gate 13." Announced John's Travel Concierge.

"Laura, I need to..."

"I know," said Laura, "Our dream team is really planning everything for us. I need to stop by a special place too. I'll see you at gate 13 in 10 minutes so we can board as soon as the gate opens. My Travel Concierge Michele just let me know we are going to board with the first group."

"I think you and Michele are building some kind of relationship! Should I be jealous?"

"Let's say that Michele and I are 'cerebrally aligned'. It must be some kind of AI technology. He knows what music I like, what food I crave, my preferred book selection... I think he even knows what I am thinking, sometimes..."

"Well, you two don't get too close. Once the trip is over, Michele is going back home. Alone!"

Laura smiled and gave him a quick kiss. "Is my quiet and reserved Scandinavian husband mutating into a jealous, hot blooded Italian? By the way, what is his ... her name? How did you call it?"

"I can't decide. I think I'll call it *IT* for now. See you in a few."

---

[11] The Bakery

John kissed Laura and walked toward *Il Forno*. The shop looked – and smelled- like an authentic Italian bakery. "So many choices!" he thought. Breads of any kind, shape and size filled the shelves on the wall. Colorful pastries and moist and decadent cookies, adorned serving plates and glass displays. Crispy, buttered croissants had a special place on marble countertop. Chocolate, marmalade, almond, honey! John had never heard of so many different filling choices.

"Buon giorno amico, come stai?"[12] An energetic and passionate man greeted him at the cash register. "Parli Italiano?"[13]

"Un pochito" replied John.

"Signor Pasquale, buon giorno!"[14] John's Travel Concierge started. "Sono pronti I cornetti?"[15]

Astonished, Pasquale looked at John's device, then he shouted to his colleague. "Listen to that, Francesca! The phone is talking to me!"

"Gesu' Pasqua', are you already drunk so early in the morning? Please stay focused," replied Francesca, a dark hair girl serving sugar-loaded cannoli to a couple of little children.

Pasquale walked to a heated display and picked up a blue and gold package. "Signore! Here are your croissants. Buon appetito e buon viaggio!"[16] He gave the package to John, then waived to the Travel Concierge "And Buon Viaggio to you too, little guy!"

"Thank you so much." John walked back toward the gate. "I really need to give you a name," he thought looking at his Travel Concierge. "I think I'll call you "Francesca." Yes. "Francesca, before I board I need to get some magazines. Is there a book store nearby?"

"Certainly John!" Replied back the device with a brand new female voice with light Italian accent. Just turn right and walk a few yards. The book

---

[12] How are you, my friend?

[13] Do you speak Italian?

[14] Mr. Pasquale, good morning

[15] Are the croissants ready?

[16] Enjoy and have a great trip

store is just after the men's restrooms. Now, I am technically not entitled to enter the gents, but you may want to stop by it as well, before departure. Just in case..."

"Thank you for the suggestion, Francesca. And do not worry. I'll keep you inside my jacket. This way you won't feel embarrassed."

"Thank you John, I guess I am lucky I can't blush." And all of the sudden a phone screen turned red.

John laughed and walked toward the bookstore... And the restrooms, feeling like he was secretly hiding something (or someone) in his jacket.

\* \* \*

"Laura, I hope you will forgive me, but I found a place you may like ... or not. Please put your headsets on and walk a few steps forward"

Laura was puzzled by what Michele had just *said*. "This is crazy," she thought, "I am listening to a phone giving me directions on what to do or not." She put on her headsets and started walking.

A song started playing. "Is that Mozart?" A slow-paced piece of classic music. Simple harmonies played by oboe, clarinet and piano. An unpretentious melody for ... children... Happy, joyful and playful children. Laura slowed down and looked in front of her. A small playground full of little children playing and chasing each other. A boy pretending to be an astronaut. A little *pirate* girl claiming her fantasy island. Two infants trying to kick a ball without falling on the ground. She could not hear the giggles and little screams of joy the little ones were sharing, but she could feel the happiness. Children of many different places and background playing all together. Mindless of anything happening in the world or just around them.

"Laura, was that a good idea? Please let me know. I am still learning your preferential patterns. If I have made a mistake, please forgive me. I shall not make the same mistake twice."

"No Michele," said Laura, crying inside. "It's ok. This is beautiful. Thank you."

"Great! I have something else for you then. Freshly squeezed lemonade is

ANGELS, LOVE, AND LOST SOULS

waiting for you. Turn left and stop by the *Blind Lemon*. Just show your ID and pick up your purchase. All has been taken care of as per your purchasing profile."

"Thank you Michele. Can you make two, while I walk? I am sure John would enjoy some refreshment before the departure as well."

"Sure, Laura! Two lemonades on their way."

Laura turned around again to look at the playground once more. Lilly would have been playing there too. She would have been a pirate. An astronaut. Maybe a ballerina twirling around the playground.

"I wonder where she is now. What is she doing? Is she safe? Does she even remember me?" Laura closed her eyes: a tear slowly marking her face. The music ended. Laura took out a napkin from her purse and started walking. "Lemonade will be great. Yes. A really great thing."

# CHAPTER XXXI

## *Minneapolis-St. Paul Airport, Minnesota*

Sebastian had finally managed to pass through the security screening. He run to the gate hoping to make it before it closed. Gasping for air, he reached the gate just in time to hear the announcement.

"Attention please, this communication is for all travelers departing to JFK from Gate 13. Due to inclement weather, our departure has been delayed by 30 minutes. Please remain nearby the Gate to hear any additional communication we may have"

"Well, at least I made it to the gate. What an ordeal!" Sebastian thought. "Next time I'll fly ahead. Just in case. Had I travelled with Gerard, this is what he would have recommended." He looked around. No sight of his customers. Good. He sat in a corner and kept sunglasses and baseball hat on to avoid any visual contact with them. He switched on his mobile phone and checked his voicemail. Only one message from Gerard -not that he had given his new number to that many people. Only his family, Fernando and Gerard knew how to get hold of him.

Sebastian dialed the number for Golden Bank Cincinnati. He needed to resolve whatever was going on with his credit card. "Thank you for calling Golden Bank Cincinnati. How may I direct your call?" said a young voice.

"I need to speak with Gloria. Mrs. Gloria McDonald, please."

"One moment please ... Sir, may I have your first and last name?"

"You can tell her Sebastian needs to talk to her. She knows me quite well."

"Sure. Just a moment. Mrs. Gloria is in a meeting right now. I hope you won't mind if I put you on hold for a minute"

"That would be ..."

"Sebastian!" screamed a voice on the other side of the phone. "Where in the Hell are you? I have been calling you for hours! You better have a good excuse. And make it a REALLY good one."

"Hi Gloria, how are you? You sound quite hysterically upset..."

"Upset? You tell ME I sound upset? You should be glad I don't live up there in the middle of the God forsaken frozen tundra. Otherwise, I'd be there, wherever you are, to kick your ass."

"Gloria! Please, why are you so angry? And by the way, I live in Minneapolis. There is no tundra nearby. And millions of people live in the area so please calm down"

"I almost called the police! Your credit card has been stolen and you don't answer your phone. Gerard doesn't answer his phone. Even at work nobody can find you. You are a VERY lucky guy if I have not called 911 yet."

"Wait. You called work?"

"What was I supposed to do? You Italian knucklehead! I had no other way to get hold of you!"

Sebastian could only imagine how many people in the office were by now wondering where he was. He had put an out of office on his mailbox and had let his manager know that he needed a few days off. But by now he could expect the most unbelievable stories were circulating around the building.

"Hallo? Anybody there?" Gloria's assertive voice took him back to reality.

"Yes, I am here. What were you talking about? Stolen credit card? What credit card?"

"The one you use to buy stuff, drink your expensive Frappuccino at Starbucks, eat dinner out, and go to the movies. Do I have to go on?"

"Got the message. But my card wasn't stolen. I have it with me right now. And for your information, I don't drink Frappuccinos. I am lactose intolerant"

"Who cares about your inability to process freaking milk! Hold on!" Gloria added her assistant to the call. "Claire! Claire, please buy me some milk whatever-name-they-are-called pills and send them to Sebastian. He can't

116

manage his finances, I can't even imagine him stopping by the Pharmacy counter."

"Gloria, I am still here. I can hear you."

"Great! That means your auditory system is still functioning. Listen, if you card wasn't stolen, then your ID must have been compromised. Which is even worst. It will take me DAYS to fix this mess. Have you been online shopping again? OH... MY... GOD!"

"Gloria, are you ok?"

"Please, please, don't tell me you still have one of those *You've-got-mail* accounts from the 90s. Those addresses get hacked all the time!"

"Stop Gloria, you are giving me a headache. No, I don't have an AOL account. No, they don't get hacked all the time and no, I am pretty sure my ID has not been stolen. Can you please tell me what is going on?"

"A headache? Just wait until you stop by Cincinnati. I'll smack you by myself with my brand new Gucci purse. That should wake you up a bit! Do you realize what is going on?"

"I am really confused. I have no idea. I was just calling you because my credit card does not work anymore."

"Thank God it does not! Somebody is charging crazy stuff on the card and it is now maxed up!"

"Maxed up?

"Kaput. Finito. Nada. You have 0 cents left on your credit availability."

"That is not possible. Are you sure, Gloria?"

"Sure? I get alerts for any unusual transaction my crazy clients make. I have a customized warning per customer and yours is Abba's "Waterloo". I got so many alerts from your account, my dog showed up dressed up in 70s jumpsuit and started barking the tune."

"No, no, you don't understand. There must be some confusion, Gloria. I just got two clients for my new company and I have made a few business purchases for them."

"Confusion? You put your underwear on inside out. That is confusion. You wear white after Labor Day. That is confusion. You serve tofu on Thanksgiving. That is confusion. You charge thirty grand to your credit card in two weeks? That is not confusion. Are you crazy? What clients are you talking about?" Gloria disconnected her assistant Claire and started talking in a more calming and lower tone.

"Sebastian, I have known you and your father for many years. You know, I am very open minded so you can tell me everything and I'll not judge you. Are you on drugs? Not a problem. I have many clients on all sorts of crap. I have a very good friend with a great rehab facility here in Cincinnati. If you don't want to come to Cincinnati, he can find us something up there in Canada. I am sure they still take dollars. Please let me help."

"Gloria! Stop! I am not in drugs and most of all, I live in the U.S. Not Canada! I really need your help. I am on my way to Italy and I need some money. I have some savings but I don't know if they are going to be enough. Can you do anything?"

"Italy! You are going to Italy! With no money and two clients to take care of. Have you thought about calling your shrink? Your podiatrist? Oh wait, what about telling your financial advisor that you opened a business and you needed a business card?"

"Do I need a business card? Can't I just use my regular credit card?"

"Oh my God! You have lost it for real. You are planning to manage your business expenses with your personal credit card? Did you miss your business 101 class at school?"

Gloria reconnected her assistant. "Claire! Claire! Please book me a flight north. I have foolish clients who need me. Where do I land, Sebastian? Is there even an airport? Claire! Claire! Book me a dog sled. And find me my fur. It is going to be bloody freezing up there."

"Gloria! Calm down. It's summer here too. Right now it's actually quite hot. And by the way, The Minneapolis/St. Paul airport is way larger than the Cincinnati one. Now, please, can you increase my credit line just a bit?"

"What's a 'bit' for you?"

"Maybe another $10,000?"

"Sure! Would you like my blood too with that? Or will a double cheeseburger be enough? I would have to LIQUIDATE some assets. Do you understand the word LIQUIDATE? It's like what happens when the ice up north will completely melt due to global warming. That, of course, is going to take some time... But in YOUR case, liquidation would just be immediate."

"Please do whatever needed. When do you think the card will work again?"

"Maybe tomorrow. I'll try to do my best. But for Heaven sake, Sebastian. Please talk to me before you do something stupid like this again, ok?"

"Sounds good. Thank you Gloria."

"You are welcome, crazy. By the way, Sebastian. Have a great trip. And call me when you come back"

"I'll do so. Bye, Gloria."

"Love you Hon!"

Sebastian switched off the phone and look at the time. Thirty minutes had passed but there was no activity at the gate. "I hope we fly soon. The lead time between this flight and the next connection is getting smaller and smaller..."

# CHAPTER XXXII

*Acireale, Sicily*

"Mum! Dad! Today we had a security drill. While I as napping, my teacher came over and told me to be quiet. She walked me outside to the playground where I played with other kids. While I was on the swing, I saw a few people in uniform talking to the headmaster. I could not understand what they were talking about but my teacher told me that they were just part of the security drill. Good night mum and dad! Good night brother and sister."

# PART VI

*Sebastian finds a new friend, a couple rediscovers a lost connection and a child brings his voice to light. Meanwhile, Gerard figures out something about his relationship ... with his phone*

# CHAPTER XXXIII

*MSP Airport, Minnesota*

Sebastian felt suddenly emotionally and physically exhausted. His initial excitement for the upcoming adventure had morphed into shattered sadness. "Maybe James and George are right," Sebastian thought. He closed his eyes and held his head with both hands like hiding from the crowd around him at Gate 13.

"Maybe I am not ready. Maybe I made a big mistake. Had I spent more time to think this through, I would have probably waited before starting operations. I should have waited to get my finances in place with Gloria, my new phone setup by Fernando. Maybe I could have bought a second phone without having to *borrow* it from Gerard. Maybe…"

"Smile, little pearl. Life, at the end of the day, is not ever so bad. And it is the only one we get." Somebody whispered in his ears.

Sebastian opened his eyes and looked up to see the silhouette of a glamorous lady moving away from him. How long had she been sitting nearby him without him noticing her? She looked… Stunning. Perfect, white Armani suit. Her blonde, curled hair topped by a small, old fashioned feathery hat. White gloves carrying a Prada hand luggage and by looking at the size of her diamond bracelet, the net worth of her overall outfit largely surpassed the value of his entire wealth -including his house and car. But most of all, what captured him was the scent she left behind. "The smell is so… peculiar. But also so familiar."

Sebastian tried to follow her walking through the crowd until she entered the Gucci store. Then he lost her.

His phone suddenly rang.

"Sebastian, where are you? I have called every single person I thought you would know. Finally, I got hold of Gloria and she gave me your new number. Man, she is so pissed with you!"

"Maarten, how are you? I so needed to hear your voice. Where are you? Still in Asia?"

"Asia? That was days ago! I got so stressed out I decided to take a mini vacation to Europe. Not sure where I am going yet. Maybe Spain or Portugal. I need some sun. What are you up to? Why is Gloria so angry?"

"Well… I may have overspent a little bit and she did not agree with my financial plan..."

"What's your financial plan?"

"I'll repay my credit card when I get paid at the end of the trip."

"You didn't take an advance payment?"

"No. I did not think it was right..."

"Oh my God. You are crazy. Didn't I tell you the golden rule?"

"Always fall on my ass?"

"No. That is rule number 2. Rule number 1 is to have an ass to fall on! Listen, you need money to make money. Lice will only make lice. You should have had some kind of pre-payment plan or maybe a pay-half-now-and-half-after-the-trip plan. You and I need to sit together and have a talk when you come back."

"I look forward to that, Maarten. I really do"

"All right. Now, I need to make a call... And maybe decide where I should go. Have fun and enjoy your trip."

"Thank you Maarten. And you as well."

"Ladies and Gentlemen, we are now boarding to JFK. Please remain seated until we call your zone. We are going to board first our Elite members..."

Sebastian checked the time. The delay was probably going to jeopardize the connection to Italy. *Am I going to make it on time to catch the next plane?*

\* \* \*

"Hi Boss! How are you?"

"Great. How is our boy doing?"

"Well, the gadgets look good but he may be in trouble. I think he is running out of cash. His credit card is maxed up, his savings are quite dry and he just got a call from his financial advisor."

"There is really nothing he can hide from you. Does he?"

"Definitely no, Boss."

"Can you do me a favor, Fernando? Actually, two."

"Sure, Boss."

"Can you link one of my accounts to his credit card? Just in case."

"Consider it done. What is the second question?"

"Stop calling me boss."

# CHAPTER XXXIV

## *MSP Airport, Minnesota*

"John, those croissants were amazing!" said Laura, showing her ticket to the flight attendant and sitting on her first class, window seat.

"Cornetti they call them in Italy, right Laura?" John took Laura's hand and kissed it.

"Oh yes, because of their horn-shaped feature." Laura smiled and caressed his hair.

"And that fresh lemonade was the perfect pairing!"

"John, do you think we'll make the connection?"

"I am not sure but let me check with my new friend." He pulled out his Travel Concierge. "Francesca, are we going to make the connection to Italy?"

"Hallo John. Unfortunaly no. Unless the other flight get delayed significantly, you will not make it on time to get through security and arrive at the gate before the plane departs."

"Francesca, what can we do then? Are we going to have to stay in New York for the night?"

"Of course not, John… Unless you really want to do so. I have already booked you to a later flight which will land in Rome just a little bit later than the original one. You initially had a 4-hour wait in Rome before your departure to Catania. With the new flight, you will still have about two and a half hour wait. Plenty of time."

"Francesca, do we have to do anything else, then?"

"No John. Just sit down, have a glass of wine –which by the way I have already ordered for you- and relax. Or read a book. Or sleep. Whatever pleases you."

"Well, then thank you Francesca!" He put his Travel Concierge in his pocket and turned to Laura. "I guess we are all set, Laura. All taken care of."

"I can't believe it," said Laura picking up her device. "I discovered this travel agency just by finding a business card on a table at a coffee shop."

"No, way! That is how I found out about it as well! I guess whoever the marketing person for Gerard and Sebastian Travels is, he or she must like coffee." John bent over to kiss Laura.

* * *

"Good afternoon sir, please take your seat. We are going to depart soon." The young steward quickly checked Sebastian's ticket and started making a few drinks for the few people in First Class.

Sebastian walked toward his seat. He quickly checked on his customers to find them holding each other hands, with eyes only for each other. "I think they are enjoying the trip. All looks great. At least for the time being".

He walked all the way to the end of the plane to find his window seat already taken by a toddler. His mother sitting in the middle seat. She looked at him "Do you mind, this is his first trip. He is so excited."

"Sure, don't worry. I prefer the aisle seat". That was a lie, of course.

As he was sitting, he noticed a sudden commotion at the entrance of the plane. The steward gasped, bringing his hands to his mouth, while the hostess abruptly turned around to check what was going on, lost her balance, and dropped a few glasses on the floor. "Thank God for plastic!" smiled Sebastian.

The Captain came out of his cabin to welcome somebody entering the plane. It seemed like... The lady! Yes. The lady who had whispered into his ear was now seating in first row. It seemed like the whole crew of the plane had stopped by to greet her.

*Who is she?* Sebastian had no idea. He closed his eyes and left the rolling of the plane take over him. "See you soon, Minneapolis".

# CHAPTER XXXV

*Acireale, Sicily*

**M**um! Dad! Today I didn't go outside after my nap. I was scared the men in uniform would be waiting for me at the fish market. I stayed at school, instead, and listened to a beautiful choir. They came from a far way land out west. One of the singers was really nice. She had short, silver hair and funny glasses. She told me her son does not live with her but in another country. A place where mountains are so high that snow covers them all year around.

The choir master taught me a new song called "bread of angels" and my teacher told me that I sounds like one of the angels painted on the walls of the school. It was a good day but I miss you all and I wish you were able to listen to me singing with the choir.

Good night mum. Good night dad. Good night brother and sister.

\* \* \*

*When lights switch off and candles burn down, little childish eyes close to dream at last. Safety is ephemeral. Refuge is just temporary. But peace is real. And that is good for now.*

*Loving words, affectionate gestures, a solid roof and a warm meal. Young life is still simple and dreams have no boundaries.*

*Eventually, the clock tower will come to life: bells calling to new beginnings. Darkness will brighten into dawn. Shadows will shift into a multitude of colors.*

# CHAPTER XXXV

*Hope will rise again.*

# CHAPTER XXXVI

"Welcome to JFK John," announced Francesca, John's Travel Concierge."

"Thank you Francesca," replied John, still uncertain on how to feel about developing some kind of personal relationship with an electronic device. "How much time do we have until next connection?"

"Just enough to leave this terminal, walk outside for a few yards, enter Terminal 1, check-in with Alitalia, pass Security screening again and get to your gate."

"John," Laura said, alarmed. Are we going to make it?"

"I am not sure." John replied concerned.

"Laura, please follow me." Said Michele, Laura's travel Concierge. "A dedicated driver will escort you and John from Terminal 2 to Terminal 1 without leaving the secure area." The device showed Laura the path across the airport property.

"That means..." Laura looked at John with large, big, hopeful eyes.

"That means," Continued Michele, "that as you don't leave the secure area, once you get inside Terminal 1, the only thing you will have to do is to walk to the Gate. And by the way, I have instructed the driver to leave you as close as possible to the departure gate to Rome."

"This is incredible! Who are you?"

"Well, according to you're the settings you have chosen for me, I am Michele, your personal Travel Concierge, provided by Gerard and Sebastian

Travels Company."

"Let's go Laura. We don't have much time." John took Laura's backpack and started walking toward their driver.

* * *

"Excuse me?"

A gentle tap on the shoulder woke up Sebastian. He opened his tired eyes to find dark-haired man talking to him, but he could not figure out what the man was saying. "Plane? What plane? Am I on a plane? To where?" What did the man in uniform want from him?

"Sir, we have docked at the gate. You must disembark at once."

"Disembark. Leave the plane…" Sebastian finally realized what was going on around him.

All passengers were quickly making their way out of the plane carrying heavy carry-on luggage, holding small lap dogs, or dragging away young screaming children.

"Delay. Connection. I need to run or I'll miss the connection to Rome." His synapses finally at work, Sebastian gathered his belongings and, as soon as he was able to get out of the plane, he rushed to the closest Departures screen. No trace of his clients. For what he knew, they may had already reached the other flight as they were seated at the very beginning of the plane. Sebastian looked hopelessly at the Departures' screen. Only 20 minutes to get to a Gate located 1.5 miles away… And in a different Terminal

"I can make it!" He thought and started running toward the Terminal's closest exit. Many other passengers seemed to rush in the same direction carrying their belongings and swearing profusely. But all of their efforts just led them to a bus stop: Terminal 1 a mere, distant mirage at the horizon. The group, now breathless, had to wait for the next shuttle. Sebastian now had just 12 minutes left until the gate closed. He started thinking about an emergency plan when the bus finally arrived. The crowd of anxious and angry travelers assaulted the vehicle.

Sebastian found himself hanging on his carry-on and his laptop in a small corner. With a series of turns, stops and sudden accelerations, the transit bus, fully loaded with anxious, and adrenaline filled human flesh finally arrived at Terminal 1. A sudden rush of distress, fatigue and anger, sprinkled with hope drove hopeful travelers to an irrational chase to whatever gate they were looking for.

Sebastian, pushed and rushed up a narrow escalator, found himself running to his flight: only a few minutes left before the closing of the Gate. He quickly checked on his belongings. Carry-on. Watch. Wallet. Phone. Laptop…

"Laptop… Where did I leave the laptop?" Alarmed, Sebastian stopped and moved away from the main area of the corridor leading to the flight to Rome just in time for not being run over from the irrational, disoriented and ready-to-fight crowd running to the next connection.

He tried to focus. "Where did I have my laptop last? He then recalled holding on the laptop on the bus. But he had no recollection on when he let it go. He run backward and down the narrow escalator. When he got to the platform, the bus had already left.

"I am toast. I'll never find the laptop. All of my files, my tracking software. All my data… It is all gone…"

"Sir?"

"What am I going to do now?" I won't be able to find out where my clients are. How am I going to follow them in case the Travel Concierges won't work? This is a disaster!"

"Sir?"

"I am a failure. This whole enterprise is a failure."

"Sir!" Someone tapped him on the shoulder. He turned around.

"Sir. Are you ok?" A security guard, quite concerned about him, was now holding his shoulders like a mother would do with her child.

"I lost it." He managed to say, covering his eyes and trying not to cry in front of a stranger.

"Lost what? Maybe we can find it." Her voice soft and calm thanks to years of training and her own experience of raising three children as a single mother.

"Laptop. I lost my laptop. I left it on the bus that just departed."

The Security guard went back to her desk and picked up something that looked like a computer bag...

"Did it look like this one?"

"Yes," replied Sebastian. "It has a travel tag. Gerard and Sebastian Travels. I am Sebastian."

"Well, well, Sebastian, this is your lucky day. A lady left it at the security desk." The security guard checked the travel tag to ensure the bag belonged to Sebastian. "She did not leave her name... But wow! She was stunning and she smelled like the French Riviera." She gave him the computer bag and pointed to the Departure sign. "You are really lucky. Now, go find your next connection and have a great flight... Wherever you are going."

"Did she say anything?" asked Sebastian

"Nothing... Wait! Yes, she told me to tell you that life, at the end of the day, is not ever so bad. And it is the only one we get."

Sebastian held the laptop to his nose. "Yes, the fragrance. It was her. My Guardian Angel." If he only could figure out who she was...

Now confident that he had lost his connection, Sebastian did not run to the gate. Instead, he went to the airline company's transfer desk, hoping to get a seat on the next flight to Rome. He approached the first available representative. "Good evening madam, I missed the connection for my flight to Italy. Can you help me find a seat on the next flight?"

"You should have come to the airport earlier. Don't you know the policy? You must be here two hours before departure!" said the representative, clearly disappointed she had to take care of another annoying customer.

"I am sorry, but it is not my fault. The flight from Minneapolis was delayed. Doesn't the airline company automatically book the clients to the next flight? At the end of the day I purchased a ticket to Italy. Not to JFK."

"No we don't. Your flight from Minneapolis was a Delta flight. You are now leaving with Alitalia."

"Aren't the two companies together?"

"Yes and no. Our systems do not work together. We are just partner companies. Let me see what I can do." The representative started dialing a number and put on a headset. Sebastian could see her tapping on the terminal and humming now and then on the phone. After what felt like a long time of humming and typing, the representative handed Sebastian his new reservation.

"Here it is. Your luggage is already on its way to Rome and then Catania. You may be able to find it tomorrow in Catania… Hopefully. Here is your new reservation. You need to run to the Alitalia Terminal. And be fast! You only have less than 1 hour to get on the next flight. And that is the last one for tonight."

"Oh, thank you. But what about my luggage? Isn't the policy that luggage should only fly with the passenger?"

"Do you see me making policies? I only make bookings. Oh My! Look how late it is! My shift is over. Time to go to my date!"

"Wait!" Sebastian tried to stop the representative, now walking away from the Transfers desk. "My reservation does not have a ticket with a seat!"

"That is just a reservation. You need to stop by the Alitalia desk and get a new ticket."

"I thought you were on the phone with Alitalia team!"

"I tried to talk to them, but nobody answered. I then called my date. He is waiting outside to pick me up and go to dinner. Follow directions to the Terminal. Goodbye and good luck!" And so she left. As fast as she could. Her mind already set to a wonderful dinner with her latest swipe on Tinder.

"One hour." Sebastian thought. "I can make it."

He started running again, adrenaline gushing in his veins. He passed by the same stores and restaurants he had rushed by before, went down the same narrow escalator he had run twice in the past hour, and greeted the Security guard who had found his laptop –she smiled back thinking that she had just collected a new fun memory to share at time of retirement. He jumped to the same bus he had taken before to drive back to the Terminal he had landed in from Minneapolis. But this time he had to leave the secure area and walk on a narrow street to the next terminal hugging his laptop like it was his most precious belonging in the entire world.

There were three representatives working at the Alitalia desk. Two were busy with a few customers who looked desperate. Children were crying. Some passengers were sobbing. Others were cursing. He approached Manuela, the only agent available. She looked at him and breathed slowly. Like she was getting ready to face a storm.

"How may I help you sir?"

"My flight from Minneapolis was delayed and I missed the connection to Italy. I have a new reservation but I need a new ticket to get on the last Alitalia flight to Rome."

"Would you mind giving me your reservation?"

Sebastian handed over his paperwork, hopeful that for once luck was on his side.

"I see..." Said the agent, looking for the right words.

"The representative at the Delta desk has made a reservation but she did not book the seat. The flight is oversold. I am really sorry."

"Oversold? What does that mean?"

"We don't have any more seats. Those other passengers are in your same situation." Manuela pointed to a family of five nearby. "You will have to overnight at the airport ... I can only book you on tomorrow's flight."

"But that would be too late. My luggage is already on the other flight. My clients are already on their way to Rome... There has to be another way."

"I am really sorry..."

"Manuela! " The customer representative assisting the couple with three children called.

"We were able to release 7 seats. Two were taken by Fabiola, over there."

"Great! I can accommodate my customer then!" Manuela said to the colleague. Hope brightened Sebastian's face.

"Well, if you take one, I'll only have four for my family. They are five. I need all the seats..."

Manuela looked at Sebastian. Sebastian looked back to Manuela, closed his eyes and with his head motioned to Manuela to give his seat to the family. The children screamed with joy. Husband and wife held each other. Sebastian, overwhelmed, sat on the floor.

"What time is the first flight to Italy tomorrow?

"It will be at…" Manuela gasped and at loss of words looked around searching for help from her colleagues. It was a futile attempt. The whole Alitalia team seemed frozen and unable to move.

"Well… Destiny!"

"Madam! What can I do for you?" Manuela asked, forgetting about the fact that she was already taking care of Sebastian.

Sebastian saw her Guardian Angel approaching the desk and talking with Manuela. Manuela went back to her supervisor, then tapped on her computer screen and printed out a ticket. His Angel left. Leaving behind the inebriating scent Sebastian now would have recognized anywhere.

"Sir!" Manuela announced. "Here is your ticket. Please run to Security. You don't have much time!"

"Wait. I thought you didn't have any seat left."

"We did. The "Divina"! Oh my! I can't believe I talked to her! I won't be able to sleep for days! The "Divina", has given you her seat in First Class. She saw you giving your seat to the family and decided to reward you. Please go to the gate!"

"But what about her?"

"She decided to fly to Paris instead," replied Manuela. "She will land in Rome tomorrow night with a different flight."

"Who is she?"

"You don't know her? Martina Valucelli! EVERYBODY in Italy knows her! But nobody knows where she is from. She is an actress and a jet setter. We all know her as "Martina la Divina".

Sebastian thanked Manuela and rushed to the Security lines. He made it on time to catch his connection to Italy. For the first time in his life, he found himself in First Class. There were so many things he wanted to experience as a First-Class passenger! But as he sat on his seat/couch/bed, he could not remember any. He simply fell asleep. And he dreamt. He dreamt of places far way. Of colors never seen before. Of smells – a specific one- he would never forget.

# CHAPTER XXXVII

## *Shorewood, Minnesota*

Gerard woke up from a long afternoon nap. He stretched slowly on his king size, four post bed "I really needed it. With all the madness of the move, my crazy work, Sebastian driving me insane with his business idea..." He looked outside the window: tall green trees languidly swaying to the whims of the western breeze. "I needed a break. My head was spinning."

Slowing gathering his thoughts, Gerard tried to think about the last time he had used his personal phone. "Where was I?" True. He did not have that many people to call beyond his family –and the calls to them where quite rare indeed. But still, he needed his personal phone. At least to check what was going on in the world and what his friends were doing. He remembered using it at work once to answer one Sebastian's questions regarding his LLC. But, other than that, he could not remember. Most of the people he knew had always used his work phone as that was the only phone he would answer to. He walked downstairs to check if he had left it somewhere on the first floor. He searched in every room he had been and opened every drawer he could find.

*Darn, where did I leave it? Maybe Sebastian has seen it but by now he should be on a flight to Italy.*

He went to the kitchen to get some water and noticed a post it on the refrigerator. It was a note from Sebastian. He had left him phone number and address of Fernando Aguirre, the tech guru who had coded the Travel

Assistant. "Call him for anything you may need," the note stated.

He put on some trainer pants and a t-shirt.

*I wonder if that genius of Fernando, as Sebastian calls him, can help me track my phone before the battery runs out. Besides, he has already hacked it once. He should be able to figure out something.*

He went down the stairs, opened the front door, and walked down the street. *Thank God he leaves nearby.*

Fernando opened the front door before Gerard could even ring the doorbell. "Hi, I live a few doors up with Sebastian…"

"Gerard! Of course! Sebastian talks about you all the time. How can help you?"

"Can you help me check where my phone is right now?"

"Of course. Of course… Please do come in." Fernando motioned Gerard to follow him. A small, black snoodle following them.

"I always know where it is, but this time…"

"I know, it happens all the time. We get so comfortable with our daily routines that when external changes affect our lives, we just go bonkers. Come in, come in."

Gerard did not really understand what Fernando was hinting, but he followed him anyway to a room filled with technology devices, large computer screens, and gadget he had never seen in his life.

"Here is my tracking dashboard. Have a seat." Fernando pointed Gerard to a comfortable, antique leather chair. "If all my calculations are correct… " Fernando typed on his device and went through a few screens. "Let me check where the pointer goes… There it is!" He turned the computer screen to Gerard and pointed to a red dot. "It is exactly where it should be at this moment, according to the schedule."

"Schedule? What schedule? I just lost my phone," Gerard replied perplexed. "I don't understand. What is all that blue stuff? Is my phone on Lake Minnetonka?"

"Oh no, George, you are so funny. The international flight has left JFK hours ago. That is definitely not Lake Minnetonka."

"What is it then?"

"Sea."

"What are you talking about? I didn't go to the beach lately. What is my phone doing under the sea?"

"Not UNDER, Gerard. ABOVE"

"ABOVE the sea?"

"Yes!"

"I still do not understand. Is my phone flying?"

"Oh you are so funny! I still can't believe you gave your phone to Sebastian. I would have never trusted that crazy guy. I love him, I truly do. But sometimes..."

"I never gave my phone to Sebastian. I just lost it..." Gerard replied in his mind a few conversations he had with Gerard. "Wait! Sebastian is travelling to Europe with his customers. Does he have my phone?"

"Oh, not at all!"

"Oh. Fernando you are really scaring me. Can you please just tell me where my phone is?"

"The phone is on the way to Italy as Sebastian is. But not WITH Sebastian"

"Where. Is. My. Phone. Fernando?"

"Laura has it."

"Laura who?"

"Sebastian's client. Laura."

"And she is on a plane to Italy"

"Yes."

"With my phone?"

"Yes!"

"I am going to kill the man!"

"Fernando started laughing so loud that his little dog started barking."

"Just wait till I get hold of him!" Said Gerard. "Just wait!" And with that, he left Fernando's house. Fernando still laughing hard...

# PART VII

*Sebastian finds a new friend, a couple rediscovers a lost connection and a child brings his voice to light. Meanwhile, Gerard figures out something about his relationship ... with his phone*

# CHAPTER XXXVIII

*Atlantic Ocean*

"Honey, did you enjoy your dinner?" said John filling up Laura's wine glass with bubbling Frappato.

"It was delicious! I don't know how these two devices, Michele and Francesca, do it. But they seem to anticipate every desire we have. I think we were the only two people to get personalized menus on the plane. And the wine! Who knew such wines were available on board?"

"Well, whoever designed them did a really good job." John looked at the light-red color wine that smelled (and tasted) like an explosion of cherries, fresh fruits and spices. "What are you going to do next? Shall we play some games?" He sipped the wine enjoying it fully. "Watch a movie?"

"I may read a few pages of my book first. Michele, my device, got me a brand new novel delivered to my seat before departure. I am really intrigued to find out what he picked for me."

"Funny, my device Francesca picked a book for me as well. But she must have figured out I don't like to read much. My book is all about landscaping and outdoor projects. Do you think she knows that I am planning to remodel our yard?"

"I don't know. But if she got hold of your internet searches and she is enabled to buy freely online …we may find a mountain of deliveries at home!"

"Hopefully not. I'll be broke! Talking about searches, Francesca has been looking at my music channels ad has picked up a few songs for me. Let me check out my customized playlist." John laughed, he passed the dinner trays to the flight attendant and put on his soundproof headsets. "The Platters. What a great music choice!" John exclaimed loudly. Laura gently elbowed him. From the look in her eyes he realized he had been too loud. He signaled her he got the message and closed his eyes.

".. *My prayer is to linger with you...*

*... At the end of the day...*

*...In a dream that's divine..."*

John let his mind drift. The trip had started with a fun surprise as both of them had the same idea of doing something special to build a new connection. They both had thought that travelling somewhere together would build a new bond; forge a new connection. Everything had gone well. At least for the time being. And thanks to the Travel Concierges every challenging situation had been sorted out before they even knew. John was hopeful that at their return back home, their lives would move in new direction. True, they may never be able to forget Lilly. But this new experience would provide them with many new memories to cherish together. And who knows, maybe with time a new baby looking for an adoptive family would come their way.

The tunes of blues playing in the background, John looked at Laura and noticed she was sleeping. She looked more beautiful than ever. The lights on the airplane had been dimmed down to allow passengers to relax and rest. Millions of stars dotted the evening sky. John, sat back and let his mind wander without boundaries.

* * *

Bathed in moonlight, miles away from home, enveloped in timeless clouds, Laura drifted away. Rolled by the rhythmic movements of the plane and enchanted by the sound of old lullabies, she dreamt of her sacred space.

She was back in her own small bay in the Mediterranean Sea. Her little hands playing with the water. Fingers testing the elasticity of the surface. Sunlight beams breaking on the water in colorful kaleidoscopic fragments.

Was that Sicily. Was that home? Maybe. Maybe not. The only thing she knew was that wherever she was, the place was safe. Her mind focused only on the water dripping down from her fingers in drops of rainbows all melting back together once they reached the surface. Their home. Their resting place.

Do all things broken find a resting place at last? Or they linger around. Disconnected. A whole conscience of many severed pieces destined to forever remain disjointed. Without a purpose? Home. Maybe home is the answer. But where is home? And what is home? Is that a place? A state of mind? A dream?

The little girl looked around. She didn't know the name of her home. She didn't know where she was. But she knew that place was hers. And hers only. As long as she held that place in her heart, she knew would be at peace. She would be whole. She would be at home.

* * *

Sebastian woke up in the middle of the night. A flight attendant stopped by to check if he needed anything and left with the promise to bring him something to drink.

"What a learning opportunity." Sebastian thought. "I guess anything that could go wrong actually went wrong." He looked under the seat in front of him. His rescued computer bag was still safe.

"I better get ready for the next leg of the trip. Can't wait to get to Pensione Mirabella and have a typical Sicilian dinner made by the owner Signora Maria. According to my father, her eggplant "Parmigiana" is the best on the island."

The flight attendant went back to Sebastian's seat carrying a tray with a hot dish, some wine and desert. "Here is something for you, sir. I hope you will like today's dinner menu. I also have a message for you". A small, lavender envelop adorned the dinner tray and… it smelled. He immediately recognized the fragrance. "It is from Ms. Valucelli," the hostess whispered to his hear.

Sebastian opened the envelope and started reading.

*My Dear,*

*I saw what you did. Leaving your seat to allow a family to travel to the next connection was a great gesture. I was touched and I hope you will enjoy your special treat. Life is too short and sometimes messy. But do enjoy every moment of it. It is never too bad. And at the end of the day, it is also the only one we get. Enjoy your trip!*

*Martina Valucelli*


Sebastian put the note aside. He wondered what her story was and if he would have ever been able to thank her in person. He ate his dinner, drank a few glasses of wine, and then powered up his computer to find out that first class seats allowed full internet and phone access. He sent a quick text message to Gerard and completed his travel app setup on both phone and computer. "I better start monitoring how my clients are doing."

...

"Everything ok?"

"Yes Boss... Or not. Something is wrong. Looks like he got your flight and I am tracking you on a different destination."

"I know, long story. He needed some special attention."

"How long are you going to babysit him?"

"If I didn't, you'd have no job, right?"

"Hmm... Good point."

"How is it going with our test *customers*?"

"All is good. They are on their way to Italy, having the time of their life."

"Remember. Monitor but not intrude. It all has to be between them and the devices."

"Got it boss!"

# CHAPTER XXXIX

*Acireale, Sicily*

In a small, ancient city, built and rebuilt multiple times by its resilient people, whom the whims of Mother Nature never crushed or dispersed, a little boy woke up. He dressed himself up, kissed his parents and siblings, and walked down a ramp of steps. Breakfast would be waiting for him on the first floor and a bright, sunny day would welcome him outside tall, wooden door carved by master wood makers many years ago. Following the smell of freshly baked bread and the sounds of a market readying for a day full of activities, young eyes would look up at a clear blue sky and start a new quest in pursuit of friendship and love.

# CHAPTER XL

## *Rome, Italy*

"Benvenuti a Roma. Welcome!" started the Italian immigration officer. "Are you visiting us for pleasure or business?"

"For pleasure," answered John while giving the passports to the immigration officer. "We are on our way to Sicily for a seven-day trip to the island."

"You will love Sicily. So much history. And you will really like the food. Make sure you get some cassata siciliana and granita. You'll remember the taste for many years to come!" The officer stamped the passports, handed them back to John, and smiled to Laura. "Here are your passports. Enjoy your stay."

"The expedited immigration process was incredible!" exclaimed Laura. No waiting in line and thanks to the pre-screening information we provided in advance, our immigration interview was as quick as drinking an Italian expresso!"

John smiled to Laura and took her hand. "That reminds me, we have GOT to get one of those little coffees served with lemon zest." John looked at Laura's tired but still brilliant blue eyes. "Follow me. I see a "bar" sign over there."

They walked to the coffee shop hand in hand, like two children exploring a new world. Laura helped John select a cornetto filled with peach preserve and navigate the multiple options of Italian coffee appellations. "You see, a "Macchiato" is coffee with just a bit of milk, while a "Cappuccino" has way more milk ... although less than "caffe' latte". Espressos, instead have no milk at all." Said Laura pointing to the state-of-the art coffee machine. "Espressos can be "Corto" or single shot, "Lungo" if you want two shots instead. You can also have an "Americano", which is coffee with some hot water ... The equivalent of a small U.S. coffee. And finally, you can have a "Caffe' Rinforzato" if you add some liquor in it!"

"Wow! I had no idea. Worse than ordering at Caribou." John ordered a single shot expresso which came into a small, Mercedes branded Italian ceramic cup. "Who knew Mercedes had coffee shop? Looks like everything is branded in Italy. Even the coffee cups!" said John sipping his expresso.

"I know," replied Laura. Think about how many people cross this terminal every day. I am sure it costs less than running an ad on TV. Plus, they even make money with this kind of advertisement platform. Brilliant!"

"So, what are we going to do? We have some time before our next connection. We could go shopping or just people watch for a while," said John checking his itinerary.

"Well, I forgot to switch on my Travel Assistant. I wonder if our two cyber tour guides have prepared anything special for us."

"Welcome to Rome Laura, your next connection will depart in approximately 2 hours and 43 minutes."

"Ops! Sorry Laura, I overestimated our waiting time," giggled John.

"Shh! Be quiet!"

"I took the liberty of booking a Spa session at the Elite Club located just a few steps from where you are right now," continued Michele, Laura's Travel Assistant. During the session, you and John will be able to enjoy shower service, a couple massage and a facial. At the Spa you will also find a travel bag with a change of clothes and a few toiletries. Please set your dirty laundry in the travel bag and leave the bag at the front desk. Your clothes will be dry cleaned and delivered to our headquarters. Your complimentary travel bags and your belongings will be delivered directly to your home."

"What do you think?" Laura looked at John quite puzzled.

"I don't think it is a joke so...I guess we can relax a bit. I would actually enjoy having a nice shower and a massage. My shoulders hurt."

"Well, let's walk over there then. I can see the entrance to the Elite Club just on our right."

Laura and John held hands and walked toward the Spa, a flood of people around them. People from all backgrounds and ways of life. Old, young, couples, singles and most of all children. So many children running all over the place. Giggling faces full of joy and excitement anxious to land in new places or just get back home to their toys, pets and treasured blankets. Laura slowed down and finally stopped. She felt intoxicated and unable to move. Her mind captured in a fog of thoughts, memories, and distant echoes of laughter and mixed feelings of exhilarating joy and unmeasurable sorrow.

"Laura, are you ok?" asked John enfolding her in his arms and searching for a glimpse of attention in her lost-in-dreams eyes.

"Yes, I am alright," lied Laura. "Let's get to the Spa. Can't wait to get a massage and put some fresh cucumbers on my eyes."

* * *

John came out of the dressing room and checked himself in a large mirror wall. The clothes chosen for him fit perfectly: White shirt, blue shorts and brand new ankle socks and shoes. The accessories included in the carry-on luggage included full toiletry, a necklace made of Sicilian lava rock, a bracelet made of small, blue and gold Caltagirone ceramic beads, hat, watch, handkerchief and sunglasses. He put his dirty laundry in the travel bag and left it to the front desk. He was checking passports and travel documentation when Laura joined him. If possible, she looked even more beautiful than ever in her long, white dress. Laces and small macramé details decorated the entire silhouette, small golden earrings and necklace to match her bracelets.

"Can you believe these clothes? I feel treated like a princess!"

"Well. You are indeed. You are my beautiful princess." John hugged her and kissed her. "So, what is next for us?"

"We still have a couple of hours. Not that we need more shopping, but what about just walking around?"

"Sounds like a great idea. Maybe we could stop by a café' for a gelato?"

148

"It's a deal!" John took Laura's hand and put on his backpack. The moment they walked out of the spa, they were both hit by the chaotic atmosphere of the airport. No more classic music and sensual smells. Just cacophonic noises and hyper-active crowds around them. John put his arm around Laura to protect her and give her a sense of security and warmth.

While John was ordering gelatos and coffees, Laura noticed a large promotional ad showcasing a variety of Sicilian attractions: lava explosions on the Etna volcano, crystal blue water surrounding the Eolian islands, baroque buildings of Noto, golden mosaics in the cathedral at Palermo and a few hotels dotting the island. One, in particular, "Hotel Delle Muse" captured her attention. Each room was different in décor and features as it was designed by a different artist.

Laura picked up her Concierge and started searching for the hotel to find out what made it so special. She found out that the hotel was actually a museum located in the middle of a network of sculptures and monuments spread around the entire valley and surrounding hills. Each room of the hotel was its own art gallery with paintings made by internationally renowned artist and furniture of the most unique materials.

"My little dreamer..." John set gelatos and coffee on a small table. "Looks like something important has captured your attention. Everything ok?"

"Oh yes. I was just fascinated by a very special hotel I found on internet."

"Laura, if the hotel is close to where we are going we can just stop by and look at the rooms. What do you think?

"That's a great idea. Looks like there is a lot of art and monuments we could look at. Oh my! This gelato is amazing! If we don't leave this airport soon we are going to be fat as pigs!"

"I wonder what our Concierges would suggest. Let me check with Francesca." John activated his device.

"John, I have synchronized my network with Michele. Looks like Laura is very interested in visiting a specific area of the island. There is a flight leaving for Palermo two gates from where you are now. I could change your reservation and put you two on it. In Palermo, I'll arrange for your transfer to the hotel and the delivery of your luggage to the new destination. Your existing hotel reservation will be cancelled. Would you like me to execute the change?"

"Do we have any other options?" Answered John.

"Sure! You can always wait where you are for about an hour and wait for your connection to Catania."

"Laura?"

* * *

Time to run again, for Sebastian. The flight to Rome had not been too late, but the taxiing on the tarmat seemed to last forever. Luckily Sebastian's seat in first class was located close to the exit door and Sebastian could sprint through the bridge connecting to the terminal without having to fight too many people. He still had dual citizenship "Thank you Dad!" so he had been able to bypass the long immigration checkpoint lines all non-European travelers had to go through, but he had barely enough time to get to his connection to Catania. Once on the plane, he was rushed to his seat. No time to check if his clients were on the same flight. "I'll check the status of the Travel Concierges once I land."

# PART VIII

*Sebastian lands in Catania, Laura and John land in Palermo and a boy is still searching for a place to land.*

# CHAPTER XLI

### *Sicily*

T he flight to Catania was really short. Sebastian only had time to drink some orange juice and take a few pictures from his window seat. "I'll never understand why you can't have coffee on the planes to Sicily. Only water and juice is available. Is coffee that expensive, and the flight that short that it is not financially rewarding to buy and serve coffee?" He perused the airline's magazine. It was full of Sicilian articles and ads, always a source of ideas for future trips. While reading, he noticed that the passenger nearby him was reading an Italian newspaper. A picture of his benefactor was on the main page. "Divina Martina lands in Paris ditching paparazzi waiting in Rome," read the headlines.

"Excuse me", he asked the passenger. "Did something happen to the lady on the main page?"

"Uh? Ah! The Divina! What a woman! Apparently she was supposed to land in Rome to attend a major event in honor of the Italian Prime Minister. All the paparazzi were waiting for her. But she showed up in Paris instead and will take a private jet to Italy later today."

"Do you think she did it to avoid the paparazzi?"

"Avoid them? She loves them! They made her what she is now. Nobody really knows anything about her. She just showed up in the Italian newspapers a couple of years ago. Since then, she has been seen only with the rich and the famous! Now, here is the interesting thing," pointing to the newspaper." According to her publicist, one of her American fans welcomed

152

her in New York City with a splendid bouquet of flowers last night." He pointed to a bunch of flowers captured on the picture of the magazine "You see, it must be the bouquet she is carrying in the picture. It almost hides her face. The story goes, she was intoxicated by the smell and before the bouquet would spoil, she had to stop by her fragrance designers in Provence to duplicate it and make it one of her signature fragrances."

"Do you think it is true?" asked Sebastian, knowing for certain that the reason of the change in plans was that he had taken her seat –the last one available on the last plane to Rome.

"Who knows? I wonder..." the passenger brought the newspaper closer to his face, "Maybe she is hiding her face because she just had a new plastic surgery? Nah. She is too beautiful."

Sebastian turned his sight to his window. The best part of the flight to the Island came when the plane flew over the Eolian islands and Mount Etna. The small islands looked like gleaming pearls on cobalt blue silk. Just a few miles south, the volcano always guaranteed the views of spectacular lava falls and luscious, green forests dotted by iron red, ancient calderas.

Flight 23 landed on time in Catania. It had been a long and stressful journey, but he was finally in a place he knew. He had a large network of people to rely on, thanks to his father's connections, and his knowledge of the Italian language –which he had practiced with his father since he was a little baby.

Giuseppe Colapesce, taxi driver by day, chef by night, was an old schoolmate of his father: with his salt and pepper hair tamed under a cherry red hat, olive skin, mozzarella white teeth, brown kakis, and basil green shirt, Giuseppe welcomed Sebastian to his homeland with a big hug. "Sebastian! Welcome home. You look just like a younger version of your father. Come here! It's hot as hell. The air conditioning in the car is broken but we can keep the windows open to get some fresh air."

"That is... great!" answered Sebastian. Not really eager to spend the next 45 minutes in a car with no air conditioning while the temperature outside was way beyond 100F. But once in the car, he immediately forgot about the temperature. Giuseppe's driving style (or speed) was very *dynamic* to say the least.

"It's a question of survival!" Giuseppe had told him. "Either you speed and drive faster than the others or you risk getting in an accident with another car."

"But if you all speed," said Sebastian "What's the point? You are all speeding toward an inevitable, deadly crash!"

"Life is short. We all die anyway. But not today. Sit back and relax." Giuseppe switched on Satellite radio settled on 70's hits. Abba's *Mamma Mia* could not be a more appropriate song for a car racing through a congested freeway.

"Signora Maria is looking forward to seeing you again," screamed Giuseppe while signaling with one of his hands something not very complimentary to a driver who got too close. "Roundabouts! Nobody knows how to drive on a roundabout. Nobody stops!"

"Isn't it best practice to slow down and wait for the car in the roundabout to pass through before getting into the roundabout?" Asked Sebastian.

"Slow down? Are you crazy? You are going to get hit!"

"I rest my case. I guess I better put my seat belt on."

"No way! What if we get in a car crash? If you can't get out of the car quickly you could die!"

Sebastian thought there was no chance of winning with Giuseppe. He held on to his backpack and hoped for the best. When he finally arrived at the Pensione Mirabella, Signora Maria was waiting for him outside the front door.

"Bastiano! Come here!" He would never get used to how his name sounded in Sicilian. "You look like you have not eaten for month! You used to look so happy![17] Now you are so skinny! You have lost your toddler curly hair and your skin color matches my white linen. You need some Sicilian sun and a lot of my food! Come in, come in." She gave him a big hug and shoved him inside the hotel. Inside the lobby, the cold of the air of the A/C hit Sebastian like a sudden slap on his face.

---

[17] Sicilian way to state that a person is plump

"Ah! Now I can breathe again!" Exclaimed Signora Maria. "It's so hot outside! You could not choose a worse time of the year to come to Sicily. Anyway, I am glad you are finally here. This is your key. My best room is ready for you. Freshen up and get changed for dinner. Mind you. Your shorts are not welcome at the table after 6:00 p.m. Go! Go!" Signora Maria hushed Sebastian toward a corridor.

Sebastian felt like his mum had just welcomed him home and scolded him at the same time.

"And before I forget," screamed Donna Maria from the Reception, "I made my special eggplant Parmisan, just as your father liked it. I am sure it will help you remember me when you go back to the United States."

Both walls of the corridor were covered with family portraits and pictures of people he did not recognize. Once he got to his room, as he inserted the key into the door, a photograph captured his attention. Three smiling people were staring at him just on the left side of the doorframe. He couldn't believe it at first, but there was no doubt: it was his family. A younger version of his father was holding his mother in a loving embrace while toddler Sebastian was looking up, smiling at his parents. "How is it possible?"

The room was nothing special in décor and furniture -it was actually the smallest room in the building. But the screen window opened directly to the beach. As Sebastian would find out the following day, at sunrise there was no other place on earth Sebastian would have wanted to be-as the sun slowly took its place above the horizon, sky and sea would became the stage of a burst of light and colors.

He quickly showered and put on some clean clothes. No shorts, or flip flaps or short sleeves shirt. Signora Maria would have sent him back to his room to get changed.

"Come! Have a seat," Signora Maria welcomed him to the dining room. *La vie en Rose*, Signora Maria's favorite song, echoed in the room. "I made a couple of things for you. A few of starters with caponata, pecorino cheese, salami, olives and prosciutto di Parma rolled over white melon. A little bit of pasta with my homemade tomato sauce topped by eggplant and parmesan cheese, a simple salad with fennel and oranges, tuna with onion and peas, roasted baby potatoes, my special eggplant Parmesan, and a couple of cannoli as desert. I set out some homemade bread as well, and a bottle of iced white wine. Would you like anything more?"

"More?" replied Sebastian just wondering how he would manage to eat everything just to please Signora Maria. "I think this will be enough for a family of four! Quick question. What is the reason for playing French songs in your Sicilian restaurant?"

"Why? Don't you Americans play Italian music in American restaurants? So what? Can't I play French songs in my Italian Pensione? It reminds me of a great time in my life. I like playing it, every once a while ... And I play Sicilian and Italian songs too...Now eat! I'll join you after dinner." Signora Maria went back to the kitchen to prepare more delicious dishes for her clients. Sebastian screened the room. No trace of his customers. "Maybe they are taking a well-deserved nap after a long trip."

Pensione Mirabella was not a fancy place. But with time it had acquired a certain reputation for the quality of its food and the colorful and caring customer service provided by Signora Maria and her family.

Sebastian tried to sample as many dishes as he could. All around him, guests were enjoying their meals as well. Some people shared stories, young couples fed their children, while single travelers enjoyed a book or take pictures of their just-delivered dishes. "How are you liking your dinner?" Signora Maria asked.

"Delicious. Just perfect. I wish I could eat it all!"

"Oh, don't worry, Sebastian. Eat as much as you can, there will always be more tomorrow." Smiled Signora Maria.

"I have a question, Signora Maria. Did another American couple check in this afternoon? They left Minneapolis with my same flight." Sebastian dove once again into a multi-layered eggplant Parmisan and let its Mediterranean juice and flavors overwhelm his senses.

"There was a couple booked from Minneapolis. I had a great suite reserved for them but they canceled this morning."

The delicious treat he was enjoying just a few seconds earlier, all of a sudden went to the wrong *pipe* and Sebastian started coughing violently.

"Mamma mia!" screamed Signora Lucia. "Mario! Mario! Come here! Help me!" Mario, the chef, ran out of the kitchen and gave Sebastian the Heimlich. Signora Maria filled a glass with water and offered it to Sebastian. "Everything ok?"

"Yes, yes," he managed to reply. "I just need to get to my room and make a call."

"Have some rest. You look dreadful. You should really think about moving to Sicily. Lots of sun, good food and nice girls. Now, go to your room! Go! Before you scare me again."

Sebastian went back to his room. As he started to open the door, he looked to his left. The picture with his family was gone. "Did I imagine it?" He quickly powered up his laptop and opened his Travel Concierge monitoring system: no trace of his clients. He reached out to his phone, finally charged and quickly dialed Fernando in Minneapolis.

"Sebastian! Do you know what time it is? Are you ok?"

"I am really sorry Fernando, I forgot about the time zones. I need your help. I can't find my clients and my Travel Concierge monitoring system is not working. Can you track them down?"

"I don't have to. I already know where they are. I thought you knew that as well."

"No, I don't. They were supposed to be at the Pensione Mirabella nearby Catania but they cancelled the reservation and I lost them."

"They didn't cancel the reservation."

"What are you talking about? They are not here. I am sure."

"Of course they are not there. The reservation was cancelled."

"Look, "Sebastian was getting exasperated. "Don't play games with me. If they did not cancel the reservation, but the reservation was cancelled, who cancelled it?"

"Not who, but what."

"What are you talking about?"

"The devices cancelled the reservation."

"What? I did not know they could do that! How?"

"They are constantly learning about Laura and John. As they learn, they adapt to what Laura and John like or need. Somewhere in Rome, Laura started searching for a special hotel in Sicily and the devices caught the new behavior."

"Are you telling me the devices noticed Laura making a search and cancelled the reservation?"

"Of course not! They are not that clever. At least not yet...but they provided Laura and John with something you and I did not plan for."

"Like?"

"A choice. They provided Laura and John with two alternatives and Laura decided that going somewhere else was a better alternative than what you had scheduled for them. Once the change in plan was made, I got a notification. You would have too, had you had a Travel Concierge app on your phone."

"You have one?"

"Of course I do. I have the first prototype. Everything I build and test is on my own phone."

"I should have thought about it. So where are they now?"

"Let me check." Fernando pulled up the Travel Concierge app on his phone. "They are at the Hotel Delle Muse. Laura rented a car after landing in Palermo and drove to the hotel."

"Palermo? That is on the opposite side of the island from where I am now!"

"Yes, the devices rebooked Laura and John on an earlier flight to Palermo. Didn't you notice they were not on your flight?"

"No, I had a very adventurous journey, to say the least... Thank you Fernando. I'll rent a car tomorrow and drive to the new hotel. Have a good night."

"I will, as long as you don't wake me up again! Good night, crazy."

\* \* \*

"Did you..."

"Yes, I removed the picture."

"I totally forgot it was still hanging nearby the room they occupied the last time they were here. How stupid of me."

"Don't cry, mum. It's ok. I am sure he didn't notice it."

"This could be my last chance to fix it. I can't mess it up."

"All will be fine. Don't worry."

"I hope so."

* * *

(Whispering voice singing inside a church)

A smile is just a smile

A hug is just a hug

A kiss is just a kiss

But a family is everything

# CHAPTER XLII

*Palermo, Sicily*

"Welcome to Palermo!" announced Francesca, John's Travel Concierge. "Please follow directions to the exit. Your rental car is already waiting for you outside the airport."

John and Laura walked through the airport all the way to the exit door: a driver in uniform waiting for them with a Gerard and Sebastian Travels sign. "Please follow me", he said, "Your car is waiting. I am really sorry but I wasn't able to find an automatic car for you. Availability of such cars is very limited in Italy. But you will really like your vehicle. It is the latest model.

Very efficient. You will not have to stop by the gas stations that much."

The driver escorted them outside the airport. They walked to a small parking lot to find a brand new Jaguar waiting for them. "Have you..." started Laura.

"I must have been perusing a few Jaguar sites during the flight..." replied John scratching his head, "I need to start being careful on how I use my device or this trip is going to cost me a fortune!"

John started walking to the driver's side of the car when Laura stopped him. "My country, my drive. You will never survive driving in Palermo."

"But Laura, you were only a child last time you were in Italy. What do you know about driving on the island?"

"It comes with your DNA. It is in my blood. Captive lionesses living most of their lives in a zoo still remain lionesses. Take them back to the jungle and you better get out of their way." She at the driver's seat and switched on the engine. "Put your seatbelt on and get ready for the ride of your life ... or FOR your life. A lady driving a convertible Jaguar in Palermo? We are going to have all the attention. Everybody will want to race us."

"What if we get stopped by the police?"

"Well, we better not!"

Laura drove through cities, villages and landmarks the names of which she could not remember. But she felt that the environment was familiar. Fragments of Sicilian history came back to her mind. She could see her father sitting on her bed reading tales from an ancient past. A noble woman killed by a jealous husband. The Norman capital city ruled by Swedish kings. The ancient Greek fortress founded hundreds of years before Jesus was even born. Laura bathed in the sun shining strong and bright above her. She drove through the wind breaking on the window shield. She felt energized and strong. Intoxicated. At home.

"Please take the next exit on the right. Hotel Delle Muse is just a couple of miles away." Breaking the spell in which Laura and John had been caught in, Michele, the Travel Concierge, helped Laura navigate the net of small streets, curves and corners that took them to the final destination. Hotel Delle Muse was a tall building set on a picturesque rock beach. Its white stone exterior shone against a crisp blue sea that merged with the sky in the distant horizon.

"It looks like a castle in a magic land," murmured Laura softly. She didn't want to break the enchantment. John put his arm around Laura's shoulder and kissed her on her forehead. "You are always right. This was a great choice. Can't wait to see what it looks like inside."

He jumped off the car, got the backpacks and opened Laura's door. The two held hands while walking into their enchanted palace.

# CHAPTER XLIII

*East Coast of Sicily*

L eaving Pensione Mirabella had been tough. Signora Maria had let Sebastian go only after he had promised her to stop by before flying back to the United States. Hugs and kisses later, Sebastian was on the road to his clients. That sliver of land captured between the sea and the snow-capped Mountain Etna was the part of the Sicily he loved the most. Green. Luscious. Vibrant and full of life. Never too cold or too hot. Packed full of loving people. "I could retire here one day." Sebastian thought, as he looked at seagulls dancing on the horizon. The southernmost tip of the Italian peninsula peeked at him from a distance.

Sebastian arrived at the Hotel Delle Muse early in the afternoon. He approached the front desk to check if there was any room available.

"Our most popular room, *The Nest* has been already taken by a lovely couple. I am sorry. They are Americans like you. And from Minnesota as well! But I have a couple of very nice rooms available. Would you like me to show you around?"

"Why don't you surprise me? I'll take the room you like the most instead. I'll take a walk to the beach while you get the room ready. I am in no hurry."

"Sure. I'll take care of your luggage Mr. Sebastian."

He walked out of the hotel. The beach was made of small pebbles that tickled his feet. Here and there, large rocks reached out to the sea. Sitting on one of the rocks, looking out into the horizon, there was a figure that seemed familiar to him. Long, blond hair blown by the sea breeze. A white,

163

long dress rippled around her frame. Stiletto heels -so out of context- in her left hand while her right hand played with the water as small waves crashed underneath the rock.

He wanted to get closer. "Could she be… No, it's not possible. She is in France. How would she even know about this place?"

"Signor Sebastian!" A voice called him from the hotel. "Your room is ready. You'll be very satisfied. I am sure."

The curator guided Sebastian through floors, corridors and staircases. She finally opened a solid, wooden door. Sebastian followed the curator into a room designed for a Middle Eastern prince. Multicolored glass windows that reminded him the feathers of a beautiful male peacock filtered the sunlight coming from outside dimming it down to a warm tone that matched the burnt orange of walls and tiled floors. He could see a green marbled bath tab, shaped like the Star of David in the next room.

"What's behind that other door?" He asked the curator pointing to a second, colossal, mahogany door.

"That is the feature that gives the name to the room. A Turkish bath. This room is perfect for travelers in need of rest and restore. And you look like you may need some, if I may. Do you like this room?"

"Yes, replied Sebastian. This is perfect. Thank you."

The curator smiled. "Another satisfied customer, then." She left Sebastian wandering around in admiration.

\* \* \*

"Mum! Dad! Today a group of singers came over. Their voices were beautiful! I sang for them and they taught me new songs. I wish you could hear us singing! Good night mum and dad. Good night little brother and big sister."

# CHAPTER XLIV

## *Castel di Tusa, Messina, Sicily*

Sunbeams glistened on the water. Sparkles of light danced slowly through the window. Laura woke up and looked through a small opening to the open sea.

*The Nest* she had called it. The manager, more a curator of an art gallery than the executive of a hotel, had showed them many different rooms. A wooden life boat bed floating on a sea-blue flooring. Sensual, warm, red lights flooding a simple space: fluorescent lights projecting furtive messages on floating, ethereal surfaces. A ceiling opening the bedroom to a star crowded sky. A labyrinth of mirrors leading to alcoves of hay and dirt. Waterfalls and magic sea creatures. The hotel was a place where reality, time and space had no meaning.

The very last room the curator had showed them was very simple. White walls and floors. No furniture at all. A colossal, wooden feature filled most the room.

"What is that?" Laura had asked.

"This is our most requested room." The curator smiled. "Try to walk around it."

Laura had carefully touched the artifact. Warm. Solid. Ancient. She had slowly walked around to find a small opening.

"I don't understand..."

"Try to get into it and tell me what you feel." The curator dimmed down the lights.

Laura remembered removing her shoes and entering a sacred space to find herself sitting on white, soft linens embroidered with little pieces of fabric resembling...

"Feathers!"

"Yes. You would be sleeping on a bed of feathers. What else do you notice?"

From the outside, the walls of the art piece looked sterile, simple. But looking at them from inside, they felt different.

"One of the walls is shorter than the other one."

"How do you feel?"

"I feel enfolded. Protected. It feels like being in a...nest!"

"Exactly. The walls are the wings protecting the eggs."

Laura had looked through the small opening. That sliver of universe resembled everything a little bird would know of the world until it would leave the nest and the protective eye of its mother. She started to cry.

"Laura! Are you ok?" John had rushed to hold her hand.

"Yes. This is beautiful. Can we stay here for the night?"

"Of course," had said the Curator. "I'll take care of everything."

"Thank you," Laura had replied from inside the nest.

As the sun rose at the horizon, Laura felt again the void of not being able to ever become the protective wing of her offspring. Her home was safe, solid, and full of love. But it wasn't a nest. Nobody to teach how the world works. Nobody to lead to a new path. Nobody to be enchanted on a daily basis. A sudden kiss took her mind back to the soft, feathery covers.

"I absolutely love the idea to sleep in a nest a rest on a bed shaped as an egg but... I feel like my back could benefit from a night spent in a more traditional, rectangular-shape furniture," said John playing with her long, curly hair.

"You're right. Let's get some breakfast. Time to explore the hills. I read that they are dotted with sculptures and monuments. Just give me a minute to enjoy the view from our little nest."

Laura sat at the end of the bed and looked outside. "Just one more minute." She thought. "Just one more minute."

* * *

"Dad?"

"Sebastian, aren't you in Italy? Everything ok?

"Yes. Everything is fine. Hope I didn't wake you up."

"Not at all. I was planning to finish a few pages before going to bed."

"Dad, I have a crazy question."

"Go on, Sebastian."

"First of all, thank you for referring me to Signora Maria. I had completely forgotten about Pensione Mirabella. The hotel is small but really cute. And the food! Signora Maria spoiled me."

"I am glad you liked it. We used to go there quite frequently when you were little."

"With that said, I feel there is something more…"

"What do you mean, Sebastian."

"When I got to my room, I could swear I saw a picture of us. I mean, a picture of the two of us and mum."

"Are you sure, Sebastian?"

"Well… Yes and no. When I went back to check on it, the picture was not there anymore… Maybe I just imagined it all."

"Maybe you are correct."

"Dad?"

"Yes, Sebastian."

"Why is that you have no family pictures of you in Italy? I'll rephrase it. I saw pictures of you and various people, including mum. But you have never showed me your Italian parents."

"You know that they died when I was very young, Sebastian."

"I know. But how is it possible you have no pictures of them?"

"I guess I did, but as I moved from relative to relative, they must have gotten lost."

"Hmm… I guess that makes sense. Sorry for bothering you, dad."

"No worries, call me any time. Now, go back to bed. It must be very early over there. You need some sleep to catch up with jetlag."

"Yes, you are right. Buona notte[18], papa'"

"Buona note Sebastian."

---

# PART IX

*Laura and John enjoy a meal... or two, Sebastian eats his favorite dishes, and a grandmother feeds a starving family relation.*

# CHAPTER XLV

*Castel di Tusa, Messina, Sicily*

"Y ou are now entering the largest open-space exhibition in Europe: a collection of sculptures and monuments stretching for miles across multiple hills and ancient river beds," announced Michele.

"I don't know how I am I going to readjust to a life without Michele and Francesca after this trip." said John. "I feel like they have become part of our family."

Laura smiled and, if it was even possible, accelerated the car's speed, pushing the Jaguar to overtake any slower driver.

"I had no idea you could drive so fast, Laura."

"Michele said that it takes at least half a day to visit all the moments. We are on a race with time. And I am not going to lose."

Laura and John visited many small villages, valleys and rural settings on the Northern coast of Sicily to find all the art pieces mentioned by their Travel Concierge. They saw a colossal blue *window* overlooking the sea. They passed pyramids marking geographic landmarks. Sheep and goats watched them with curiosity while they played like children, chasing each other inside an open-air labyrinth as wide as Mall of America. Finally, Laura stopped the Jaguar near the last monumental art piece. A simple, majestic, blue sea wave set on top of a hill. Laura took off her shoes and started walking on the structure. When she reached the top, she looked around. Hills, forests, sky and the sea seemed all to merge together. Here and there, small villages dotted the landscape like islands scattered on a green ocean.

John walked up on the monument and got closer to Laura. He himself captured by the natural beauty surrounding them. He hugged Laura from behind. Two castaways floating at the edge of the word. "Are you enjoying your trip?"

"This is more than a trip, John. This is magnificent, surreal beauty. Easy to imagine why a group of artists would gather together to plot such an endeavor. Pure magic."

"I guess you are not ready yet to go back to our little nest?"

"I am ready. But we are not going back to the hotel. We are heading home."

"Home? Already?" John looked at Laura puzzled and concerned. "Anything wrong?"

"Everything is absolutely perfect. We are not going home to the United States. We are going to the place where I began. My home. I'll share with you what I remember of my little nest. No family reunion though. Not yet. I need to figure out how to reconnect with them and I am not ready for that." She smiled at John and stroked his hair. "And you are definitely not ready to meet a real, large, Sicilian family, neither!"

"Let's go then. I can't wait. I'll ask Maria to resume our reservation at Pensione Mirabella. But this time I'll drive," he said, "You and Michele will be my navigators. My internal system needs a short break or I'll end up throwing up my guts!"

Laura took a final glimpse of the landscape from her towering position on top of a surreal blue wave eternally lapping on an emerald green hilltop. For the first time in a long time she felt *connected*. Whole again. At home again.

\* \* \*

"Good morning Fernando! Did I wake you up?"

"Wake me up? It's so early I barely got to bed, Sebastian. When will you learn to calculate your time difference? It's eight hours. You currently live 8 hours in the future"

"Nonsense, I am having brunch. It can't be that early...or late at night."

"It's 3:00 a.m. in Minneapolis!"

"Why are you still awake, so late at night? Can't you sleep?"

"I WAS sleeping until I got a call!"

"What kind of call, the religious one?"

"Listen! Stop trying to be funny and just tell me what you want before I hang up on you."

"Wow. You are in a mood… It's about the Travel Concierges app. I tried to upload it on my PC but it doesn't work. The upload starts but it never ends. What could that be?"

"What speed are you on?"

"I am not on 'speed' or any other drug. I have never done drugs!"

"Please, God, help me. Sebastian! I am not talking about drugs. I am talking about upload speed."

"How do I find that out?"

"Forget about it. Let me get to my desk…"

"Where you already in bed?

"No, I usually sleep upside down, hanging from the ceiling."

"Oh my, you really are in a mood…"

Once at his desk, Fernando activated his monitoring system. "Here it is. I am looking at the server. Yes, you are trying to upload the file. But your speed is too low. You need to get to a place with high-speed connection. I told you to upload the file while you were still in the United States."

"I know, but I had no time. How do I find a place with high-speed?"

"Google it."

"Really?"

"I don't know, Sebastian. Ask the Concierge working at whatever hotel you are in."

"Well, about that… I am in a very fancy hotel. They don't have a Concierge," whispers Sebastian. "They have a curator, as if I were staying in an art gallery. I spent the night in a room full of art and guess what!"

"What?"

"There was a Turkish Bath inside my room! Isn't that crazy?"

"Not as crazy as calling me in the middle of the night. Goodbye."

"Wait! Can you help me at least locating my clients? I am trying to figure out where they are."

"Well, according to the system, they are definitely not nearby you at all. They just cancelled their reservation at 'Hotel Delle Muse'. They are in route to the East Coast of the island."

"That is where I was before!"

"Yes, and there is another thing."

"Don't tell me. They are at Pensione Mirabella!"

"Yes, Sherlock. That is the name of the hotel. Goodbye."

"Goodnight Fernando. Thank you as always... Wait! Last question. "

"What? I would really like to go back to bed before having to get up and go to work. You know? That place where we all normal people go to so we can get a living."

"The Travel Concierges. Have we trademarked them?"

"Why would we want to trademark them? Do you mean patented them?"

"Yes, I mix up the two all the time. Do we have a patent?"

"Sebastian, you don't even pay me. This is just play time for both of us."

"Does that mean no?"

"Yes."

"You mean we HAVE a patent?"

"No. I mean. Yes, we DO NOT have a patent."

"Can you look into it, Fernando? I'll pay you. Please?"

"Oh my God. You are a mess. Good night."

"Please!"

"Ok, ok, goodnight."

"Shouldn't you say "Good Morning" as it is already early in the morning in Minneapolis?"

Click.

"Wow. He really was in a mood!"

# CHAPTER XLVI

*Nebrodi Mountains, Sicily*

\* \* \*

Laura and John were driving downhill from their exploration of Sicily's northernmost mountains, when they noticed a car coming up the street. On a very narrow curve, dark smoke started coming out from the engine and the driver, probably blinded by the smoke, lost control of the vehicle. John quickly turned right and accelerated to avoid a collision. The car crashed just behind him. John stopped the car and ran to check on the passengers.

"Thank God I didn't hit you! I'm really sorry." The driver had a strong Italian accent. "Something was wrong with the car and I was trying to find a good spot to stop. The smoke got too thick and I missed the curve. I hope you two are ok."

"We are fine," John started. "But what about you? Anybody else in the car? We can call 911 or whatever the Italian equivalent is…"

"We are fine. The car though may need help."

A lady came out of the car. John stared at her. She was stunning. "She looks familiar. Have I seen her somewhere?"

"John, why don't you drive him up to the village with the Jaguar. I'll stay here with his friend," said Laura. "And stop staring at her!" she whispered.

"Yes, yes. Please come with me. There is a village not far away. I am sure we'll be able to find help. Laura, I'll be back in a few."

"Thank you so much for your help. You are very kind. I am really sorry to be an inconvenience." Then he turned around to address his companion.

"Martina, I'll be back in a few minutes with some help."

"Sure, take your time. I'll be perfectly fine."

John started the car. "I'll be back soon, Laura. Call me if you need anything."

"Drive safe," she replied and walked to the ruined car. "Hi, I am Laura, nice meeting you."

"Hi. I am Martina. Thank you so much for helping us."

"Not at all. I actually missed this one."

"Excuse me?"

"This wall is actually an artwork. The "Wall of life" is made of about 40 different terracotta works made by artists from all over the world."

"Why?" replied Martina. "Why here?"

"Maybe just to give sense to this place. So far from the sea. Distant from industries and resorts. Maybe the purpose is to give this place a meaning. Something the people of this region could be proud of and share with the rest of the world. Something that states *I am here. I am alive too.*"

"And are you?" asked Martina. "Are you feeling *alive*?"

Laura looked at her. She was beautiful. Perfect clothes. Incredible hair. A smell... Still, something was off. She could not figure out what that was.

Martina turned to the wall and started walking along it to connect with its artistic parts. "What if...instead...it was a way for them, the artists, to be remembered forever? What if they were looking for an opportunity to leave their legacy, to share their "child" with the humanity? Isn't that what we all long to do at the end of the day?"

"What?" Laura looked at Martina trying to make sense of the statement.

"Offspring. Legacy. Children. Whatever we believe will survive us and take our ideas and values one step further." Martina turned back to Laura. "Do you have children?"

"No." Laura turned to the wall. "We tried... We fostered one for a little while... What about you. Do you have children?"

"There was a time when I thought I could have a family like anybody else," started Martina, "But no, I do not have children at the moment... And as the Gods have decided, I never will. But I have a vision -well, let's call it hope- that something of me is going to move forward. Even when I am gone." Martina paused and turned to look back to the road. A group of cars was quickly driving uphill. "Even here, in the middle of nowhere, they can find me..." she said. "Laura, I need your help. Please come into the car. I'll explain."

The cars approached quickly. Drivers racing each other. The person on the passenger seat hanging outside of the window looking around: searching for something like a hound. They had cameras and video devices ready for action. "Why on Earth would she come to this abandoned place?" said one passenger to his driver. She does not seem like a person who would wonder around hills to visit some monuments set in the middle of God forsaken nowhere ..."

"Maybe she is visiting a famous friend who has a castle hidden somewhere on the hills," said the driver.

The group rushed uphill, wheels shrieking as they turned on narrow, twisting curves. They overtook slow lapas[19], and barely missed a few animals crossing the street. They passed a car crash. One of the passengers, a man wearing a baseball hat and checkered red and black flannel shirt was trying to fix something inside the hood of the car, the other was talking on her mobile phone.

"Should we stop and help?" said the driver.

"And give the chance to take the picture of a lifetime to those morons behind us? No way. Drive faster!" replied one of the passengers.

Laura looked at the cars quickly passing by and speeding uphill "I can't believe nobody stopped to help us!"

"They are paparazzi looking for a prey. They will not stop until they have found what they are looking for," said Martina closing the hood of the car. She removed the baseball hat and the shirt she had quickly put on to camouflage herself "Thank God I always bring with me some *emergency*

---

[19] Small, three-wheeler truck

clothes.

The sound of another engine approaching caught Laura's attention. "Finally! Here they come."

John was waving from a distance. To Laura, he seemed like an ancient soldier riding back home victorious at the end of a mission. John parked the car near Martina's. Another vehicle stopped just behind him.

"You got a new car?" Martina asked her driver.

"Yes. I worked out a few details with the car shop. They'll fix the car and arrange for delivery to the rental car agency. It's time I get you back to the seashore. This place has just become too *hot* for you to stay. And I am not referring to the weather."

Martina hugged Laura and gave her a business card. "Please call me if you need anything. And I mean it, Laura. Anything!"

"I will, Martina. It was nice meeting you. Come and visit us in Minneapolis some time."

"Who knows," Martina replied. "I may be there soon."

# CHAPTER XLVII

*Pensione Mirabella, Acireale, Sicily*

"Oh my God! What is this! It can't be just pasta. This is an explosion of flavors that just melts in your mouth. Delizioso!" John screamed gesticulating direction to the chef.

"John! Behave!" giggled Laura. "And by the way, pasta is feminine."

"But this is 'ravioli.' I thought that words ending with "o" were masculine?"

"Well, good point. Pasta is feminine but ravioli is masculine. I am already full and I just had appetizers and first main course. I don't know how I am going to make it through salad, fish, cheese and desert. How do Italians manage to eat this way and still remain skinny?"

"They walk a lot, I guess…"

"Would you like some more wine? I make it myself! My grandchildren come over every fall to stomp their little feet on the juicy grapes," Signora Maria said pouring more wine in the glasses without even waiting for an answer.

"How many grandchildren do you have?" John sadly looked at his last ricotta-filled raviolo covered in creamy white sauce with peas and ham and topped with fresh Parmesan cheese.

"Fifteen!"

"Fif… What!?" Laura exclaimed almost drowning in the white wine she had just gulped.

"I know! We are such a small family. Although I had six children, those stinkers didn't give me more than two grandchildren each with the exception of my youngest one, the manager here at Pensione Mirabella, Nicodemo - Nico, we call him. He was the only one who blessed me not with two, but with THREE grandchildren. Good boy!" exclaimed Signora Maria to Nico, who was greeting guests driving at the restaurant.

"If I may, how did you manage to have such a large family and still run this business?" John dove his spoon into succulent caponata.

"…My first boyfriend… Bless his heart! We met in Greece. I was on summer break, just before going to college. By the time my trip was over, I was pregnant with my first child."

Signora Maria sat with Laura and John. She bent over to get closer. "It was a scandal! I could not get back home with a baby in my belly. My parents went mad. Finally my mother came over to Greece to help me deliver my little boy. She gave me some money and a few family jewels. I sold the jewels and with the few savings I opened a small restaurant in Santorini. I worked hard and eventually I bought a small hotel… Then a second one. After a while, I reconnected with my family in Sicily, left the Greek business to my eldest child, and moved back to Sicily to open this little Pensione." Signora Maria seemed to fall into haze for a couple of minutes. Then looked back to Laura and John. "I am so happy you decided to come to my place. Do you like your room? It has the best view of the bay."

"We love it! Thank you so much." Laura alternated between sipping white wine and dipping more olive-filled bread in a small bowl filled with home-made olive oil. "Yes, the view is breathtaking but I wish we could get a little bit of fresh air from the balcony. Is it usually this hot this time of the year?" Her pasta dish completely cleaned out with a final "scarpetta", little booth-the Italian way of cleaning the plate with a piece of bread to signal they have really enjoyed the dish.

"Hot? We haven't got any rain in months! We are all DYING of heat," replied Signora Maria in a very dramatic tone. "In fact, I think I could just die right now. My poor life over in just a few seconds. Like my husband, bless his hearth! One moment he was alive, then next...dead! Kaput! Adios!"

"You first mentioned a boyfriend ... Then husband... I am so sorry to hear he is now dead. Did you marry in Greece?" offered John.

"Oh! No, no. My boyfriend... He was American like you two... We did not get married. I couldn't do that to him... Anyway, that's a long story." Signora Maria stood up "I need to check the front desk. It is almost time for afternoon naps, here in Sicily. Need to make sure my personnel is still awake. Maybe I'll get them some expressos. See you later!"

"Good..." Laura started when Nicodemo, aka Nico, delivered to the table a Silver plate full of fish.

"What... is... this?" Asked John, intoxicated by the smell.

"Nothing! Just a bit of baccala' fish with baby potatoes, capers, pine nuts, olives, onions and celery. We added a pinch of parsley, garlic and dried grapes."

"But this is a fish!"

"Yeah, it's a fish. Did you want something else? Maybe some pork or chicken?"

"No, I mean, this is a whole fish!" John could not believe his eyes.

"Mamma thought you had a long trip to get here and you may be hungry...
"

John looked at Laura.

"Well, I guess we'll skip the desert..." offered Laura.

"Oh no. You can't do that." Said Nico. "Mamma will go crazy if you don't eat her cassata. Enjoy!"

"According to my calculations," started Michele, the Travel Concierge, "based upon all the food items mentioned until now, the total amount of calories estimated is…"

Laura shut off the phone.

* * *

"Sebastiano! Welcome back. You'll be happy to know your people are finally here."

"Shhh, please Signora Maria, I don't want them to know I am here as well. I want to make sure they are having a great time."

"Well, based upon how much they are eating, they surely look fine. Go upstairs, I'll get you something for dinner. A few linguini topped by eggplants and basil, and some lamb with potatoes. And don't worry. You'll have your greens too. And your pecorino cheese. Ah! I forgot. I made homemade 'cassata'. Go! Go! Before they finish their dinner. I'll catch up with you later."

Once in his room, Sebastian started unpacking. His phone came to life "Incoming call from Maarten." Sebastian's phone announced. "Finally! My Concierge app is starting to work. Thank you Fernando!" He thought. "Maaerten, still travelling?"

"I wish! I got stuck in traffic for hours waiting for my helicopter to rescue me."

"You have your own helicopter?"

"Of course I do. Everybody has one nowadays. They are so affordable… I am surprised you don't have one."

"Well, maybe one day when my revenues get closer to yours…"

"Good try. Not a chance."

"That I can get a helicopter?"

"No, that your revenues will get closer to mine. Sorry. Listen, did you find your peeps? Where are they? Are they happy? Happy customers make more happy customers!"

"I finally found them. They are staying in one of my favorite places in Sicily, Pensione Mirabella."

"Pensione?"

"Yes, why?"

"I don't think I have ever stayed at a Pensione. Do they have internet?"

"Yes, Maarten, don't be a snob. We are in Italy!"

"As long as they are happy... Listen, need to go. The helicopter is landing. See you soon and don't screw up!"

"Thank you for the pressure Maarten. Really appreciated."

"You are welcome. Any time."

Sebastian walked toward the balcony. On the cobalt blue waters of the Mediterranean Sea, seagulls were spiraling above the fishing boats.

*I wish you were here to see this, Gerard.*

He looked at his phone and started dialing. A knock at the door broke his train of thoughts. "Signor Sebastian, Signora Maria is waiting for you. Dinner is served."

"*Certo*, of course. *Arrivo subito*, on my way." He got back into the room and left the phone on his bed. *Maybe I'll call later,* he thought.

# CHAPTER XLVIII

### *Pensione Mirabella, Acireale, Sicily*

"That was certainly a dinner I'll never forget." John stretched along a bed too small for his taste. "I love Italy but I really miss our king-size bed."

"But these pillows are so soft, John! Can we take one with us? I am sure Signora Maria will let us have one, if we ask. She is so lovely." Laura breathed in the scent of orange blossom infused into the pillows. "Can you imagine, six children, fifteen grandchildren, a few hotels in Greece, and one facility in Italy? What a life! I am such an underachiever."

"I don't know. Something does not add together. A boyfriend... Then a husband... I am starting to think that her life may have been tougher than we think."

"Maybe, John. But still..." Laura lay her head on John's chest.

"What are you going to show me today, my ancient Greek muse?"

"We are going downtown. Bring your camera. And get ready to fall in love with arts, history and..."

"Please don't tell me!"

"More fragrant, luscious, inebriating, colorful food!"

"Oh my God! Do Italians eat all the time?"

"Of course not! We also drink, talk, dream, and make love... Sometimes we do all of this at the same time."

John kissed Laura. "I can't wait to get fat then."

"Fat? Oh no, you are going to burn all of those calories. Italians don't get

183

fat until they get very, VERY old."

"And how are you planning to get me burn those calories?"

"Well, we are going to walk a lot, of course… And we are also going to exercise."

"Exercise? I don't think there is any gym in this hotel."

"No need for exercise equipment. I think we have all the equipment we need just here in this room…"

\* \* \*

"Sebastiano, how did you sleep last night?" Signora Maria asked while serving a large plate of smoked salmon and scrambled eggs served on toasts: a bowl of Greek yogurt topped with fresh honey sat nearby.

"Signora Maria, you really know how to spoil me. You know, at some point I may never leave this island!" said Sebastian sipping his espresso topped with lemon zest.

"Well, nobody can say I am not trying. There are so many beautiful Sicilian women I could introduce you to…Or men!"

"Signora Maria you are making me blush! I better get done with breakfast before my clients come downstairs."

"Don't bother to rush."

"What do you mean, have they already left?"

"Honey, I've had six children and I have followed their lives as they got me fifteen grandchildren. I never had time to get a degree in anything, but there is one thing I do know for sure. I can *read* people. Those two have gone through a very tough time. And they are now re-discovering their love for each other. Take your time with your breakfast. They will barely make lunch." Signora Maria started looking around like searching for someone. "And talking about birds in love, let me go check on Nico, before I get grandchild number 16. Ciao!"

\* \* \*

"Fernando?"

"Hi Boss, I was not expecting a call from you, today."

"Great then. I built my fortune on being unpredictable."

"I am checking the devices. All looks good. Anything else I can help you with?

"Nothing specific. I called to let you know that I am going to go *offline* for a couple of days. I need you to be more vigilant than usual."

"You are going to take a vacation? I can't think about the last time..."

"I know, I know. Long overdue. I think I am going to stay at the Hotel Delle Muse for a couple of nights more."

"Well, good for you, then! Don't worry. I'll be vigilant. Enjoy your vacation!"

"I won't be on vacation, Fernando."

"Enjoy your off-line, time then. Bye Boss."

"Thank you. And please, please stop calling me Boss!"

"Sure. Bye Ms. Valucelli!"

A phone found its place on feathered bedding. A gentle breeze lifted white rose petals here and there. Far in the distance, sailing boats dotted blue waves. Clear skies speckled with seagulls. All of it framed by two wings enfolding a soul looking for answers while protected in her coveted *nest*.

# CHAPTER XLIX

*Acireale, Sicily*

"Welcome to the very heart of this very ancient city..." announced Michele, the Travel Concierge. "Six times destroyed by earthquakes and lava falls, and six times rebuilt, this city was founded around 600 B.C. by the Greeks. Enchanted by the beauty of the landscape, the founders dedicated their city to Venus, the goddess of beauty.

Some people say that when the Romans conquered the land and became Christians, to not completely lose their connection to Venus, they completely made up a Catholic Saint, Venera, to whom they re-dedicated the city under a new religion."

"So, basically..." John said holding Laura's hand, while crossing the street leading to the Cathedral. "They made up a Saint to keep both the people who did not believe in the new religion, and the new religious leadership happy."

"It was a change for no change. The best of both worlds." Laura looked up to the sky and opened her arms wide. John looked at his muse in awe: sun kissing her skin, breeze caressing her hair. She took a deep breath then pointed to a church nearby. "Did you notice how many churches, cloisters, seminaries and Catholic schools this city has?"

"Every hour... Actually, every quarter, I can hear countless of bells chiming. There must be dozens of churches in this city."

"Close to a hundred," Laura replied. "In the olden days, families competed amongst themselves. It was a race to greatness in both life on Earth and

186

Heaven. Unless you were the first male or female in the family, almost your entire existence would be dedicated to a religious order. The larger the endowment to the Church, the higher the rank. And if you happened to be the lucky first born, as long as you donated to religious projects, your sins would be cleansed. Look at this square, for example. There are two churches in the same square... And attached to each other!"

"I guess it was their version of pay-for-play." John smiled. "Look at all those gargoyles and masks. Some of them are quite disturbing!"

"It was a way for the Church to remind people that we all die, at the end of the day. Either of natural causes or from diseases like the plague.

"Plague?" John took a few pictures. "Did the plague affect this city as well?"

"Oh yes, John. Look at that church dedicated to San Sebastian, for instance. When people started dying, they prayed to St. Sebastian to protect them and end the epidemic. The clergy coordinated a long precession, bless the whole city. The plague ended and the people dedicated the city to St. Sebastian." Laura pointed to the Cathedral of St. Sebastian. "Can you see the string of cherubs chiseled on top of the gargoils? They signal that with the power of prayer, good will triumph over evil."

"Wait a minute Laura. You just told me the city was dedicated to Venera/Venus! Isn't that some kind of a conflict of interest among saints?"

"Well, I guess even Saints have their limitations... This city has two Patron Saints One female, St. Venera/Venus and one male, St. Sebastian. I think it's just fair to have one protector of each sex." Laura's face suddenly lit up with joy. "Here it is! It still exists!"

"What?" said John searching around.

"My favorite granita place. I thought I'd never find it. Last time I went there, I was just a child. I can't wait to see your face when you'll eat the best granita in the world. Totally worth it we missed breakfast this morning."

"Considering the amount of food we ate last night, I don't think I'll need to eat until tomorrow. But with this heat, some refreshing desert would be nice."

"It's not dessert, John. It's Heaven melting in your mouth. It's pleasure mixed with guilt. It is ..."

"Ok, ok, I got it. It is going to be amazing. Let's go and get some granita. Now I am really curious to try it."

"Not yet." Laura started running toward a small street leading somewhere behind the granita shop.

"Where are you going"?

"To the fish market. Come! And be ready to take tons of pictures!"

\* \* \*

Sebastian felt that he could finally get some rest end enjoy the rest of the trip while monitoring his clients from a distance. The Travel Concierge app on his phone was finally working and he could check on their location and program changes at any time. Yes, it was hot, but summer in Minnesota is short and moody while in Sicily it's long and predictable in its length and dryness. The main street of the city, Il Corso, was lined with high-end stores with customers going in and out like busy bees in the middle of the day. "I wonder if they're visiting the stores just to find some refuge from the heat," thought Sebastian. "Air conditioning is a rare and extremely appreciated commodity in a place where temperatures are constantly above 90F for most of the year."

"Excuse me, do I know you?" A young woman called.

"I'm not sure... My father was born here, and I used to live here when I was a child ... I am Sebastian, nice meeting you."

"Sebastian! I am Lucia. Lucia Aliberti. Of course I know you. Our parents used to be very close and we spent lot of time chasing crabs down the beach many years ago."

"Now I remember! You used to call me skinny..."

"Well, I must say you 'buffed up' a bit since then. Good job! What are you up to now?"

"I work in technology in Minnesota. I am here on a business ... kind of vacation. What about you?"

"Business AND vacation? Those two words usually do not go together...

I am a lawyer. I specialize in adoptions and divorces. I love working on adoption cases. But in Italy... We have many children on our own already. Adoptions are not that frequent. Divorces, however... Plenty of them. It pays the bills. Here's my business card. Call me some time. For work or... vacation something."

"Sure! It was great seeing you again. Here is my business card. If you happen to visit the United States, come to Minnesota and visit."

"Minnesota? That sounds cold. I am an islander from the Mediterranean Sea... Italian winters are already brutal for me. But who knows... I always wanted to go on a snowmobile or a dogsled... Keep in touch, Sebastian."

"You too, Lucia."

* * *

"A chiazza, the square, or 'A Pischeria', the fish market. This is what the citizens called this commercial heart of the city" said Francesca, John's Travel Concierge. "In the past, this is where people of every social lineage came to purchase any kind of food they needed."

"It's not as big as I remembered, but the colors, the smells, the people are still vibrant." exclaimed Laura. She guided John through a maze of stands full of plump eggplants, ripe tomatoes, luscious and multicolored bunches of exotic flowers, grapes so big they looked like small apricots, and ruby red watermelons. Gigantic oranges, lemons of many varieties and so many different vegetables with names and features he'd never heard of before.

On one side of the square, a store was completely dedicated to bread. "What is this?" asked John.

"Sicily was the granary of the Roman Empire. We have a very long tradition of bread making. All of these different kinds of breads are unique to this part of the island. Should you go to a different region, you'd find a completely different range of names and shapes."

John looked at some of the names as he passed by different kinds of bread and filled his nostrils with the loaves' smell: *St. Lucy's bread*, eye-shaped to honor St. Lucy, protector of the eyesight; sfincioni, soft as velvet and coated in sugar; sesame seed covered *mafalde*. Every shelf of the store was filled with bread: olives-filled breads; rosemary-filled loaves; soft breads; hard breads; long and thin grissini and pizzas. "How do you choose?" asked John.

"We don't. We pick the first one we happen to like at that specific moment. Tomorrow we'll pick a different one... Or the same one if we liked it the previous day. Come! There's more!"

They visited stores with a multitude of cheeses, establishments selling a rainbow of cured meats and sausages where butchers displayed their best cuts. And finally...the fish market. Mussels, shrimp, anchovies, salmon, tuna, crabs, oysters, and fish of every size and color of the rainbow. The pungent odor was intoxicating. Mesmerizing. And the people! People everywhere! Laughing, arguing, talking about weather, jobs, deaths, births, children. So many children. Playing, hiding from their parents, picking on the dying fish, laughing at an octopus folding its legs on the arm of a fisherman.

Laura and John found themselves surrounded by a group of children playing "Girotondo", the Italian version of "Ring around the Rosie". "Giro, giro tondo, giro intorno al mondo (round and round we go around the World)," sang the children. "Ring around the Rosie," replied Laura and John, they too circling around holding each other's hands inside the larger loop held by the children. They spun and laughed, grown-ups and little ones, in a cacophonic and spontaneous ritual.

As suddenly as the group had formed, so it dispwersed. Youngsters' interest moved from Laura and John to the next shining object. The group leader, a boy the children called Angelo led the tribe to chase the ice-cream truck. Laura and John kissed in the middle of the square in an unapologetic moment of rekindled joy- if hundreds of people were around to witness and judge, it did not matter.

The sound of bells marking the noon hour brought them back to reality. In the distance they could hear voices singing. "A choir! Let's go listen!" Laura followed the sound of an organ. Now and then, voices joined the instrument. Tenor, soprano, alto, basss... but also trumpets and violins.

"I can't believe it," said John. "Look! This is the choir of the Episcopalian church in Excelsior. We stopped by once for their Christmas service. And now they're rehearsing in Sicily!"

"We have got to go in to say hi."

Laura run inside the church of San Michele. A statue of the Archangel welcomed them with a smile from the dome up above.

# PART X

*Laura and John find a child, Sebastian reconnects with an old "friend", and a boy discovers hope.*

# CHAPTER L

"*A**ve, ave verum corpus natum de Maria virgine ...*"
Laura and John quietly entered inside the church of St. Michael while the Excelsior Choir was rehearsing Mozart's Ave Verum.

"*Vere passum immolatum*"

They dipped their fingers in the holy water font, knelt and made the sign of the cross.

"*In cruce pro homine*"

John led Laura toward the choir.

"*Cuius latus perforatum unda fluxit and sanguine...*"

They passed by a large chapel. A golden statue of a distraught Virgin Mary stood in front of a majestic painting of Jesus on the cross. Two thieves at his sides and a soldier hitting him with a spear.

"*...Esto nobis pregustatum in mortis examine...*"

A second chapel was dedicated to Mary's Ascension to Heaven. Her precious, old portrait was made with colors manufactured from crushed gold, rubies, emeralds and sapphires. Hundreds of angels led her path toward celestial coronation.

"*In mortis examine.*"

Laura and John sat near the altar, an older lady nearby. Her eyes closed. Maybe sleeping or just enjoying the performance. Choir and instruments reached a final crescendo that signaled the end of the composition.

"Great job!" said the conductor. "Looks like we're ready for our concert."

He turned around and looked at the only three people in the audience, one of them apparently asleep.

Laura recognized the conductor and started walking toward him to introduce herself when suddenly a voice sounded from the old choir loft.

*"Laudate Dominum omnes gentes, laudate eum, omnes, omnes populi."*

"Ahhh. Finally!" exclaimed the older lady, her eyes now burning with excitement. The conductor, choir members and musicians, all looked at one another.

"Laura!" John murmured, taking her hand.

*"Quoniam confirmata est, super nos Misericordia eius".*

The young voice continued singing without any instrumental support. Just pure, angelic melody.

"I have never heard anything like that. Who can..."

*"Et veritas Domini manet in aeternum"*

The conductor looked at his choir and started directing players and singers to join the singing child.

*"Gloria Patri et Spiritui Sancto.  Sicut erat in principio, et nunc, et semper. Et in saecula saeculorum."*

By the time the child sang the ending "Amen", everyone was crying. Silence suddenly followed, the sound of little feet rushing out of the church. It was like something magic had abruptly come to an end. The older lady stood up and walked outside. Laura noticed that on her way out, the lady had left a small package on the very last bench.

"Hi! I think I recognize you." My name is Andrew, said the choir director.

"Hi. I am John. My wife Laura and I are vacationing in Sicily. We are both from Chanhassen, Minnesota."

"I thought I'd seen you somewhere, maybe at church.  We come from Excelsior, Minnesota."

"Possibly," replied John. "We came for mass at Christmas, but the church was packed. There's no way you noticed us... Your choir is amazing. And that child! I don't know where you found him. He is really special!"

"Actually... He found us. I don't know who he is. I'm as astonished as you are. I met him a few days ago and he has been shadowing our rehearsals every day. I wish he could join us for the concert … Who knows?" He turned to his team, noticing their attention was starting to wander. "If you will excuse me, I need to get back to my choir. We still have a lot of work to do before we can call it a day. I hope you'll join us for the concert."

"I will… If I can find my wife." John shook the conductor's hand and rushed out of the church trying to find Laura.

\* \* \*

"Careful, little boy, you'll get hurt!" said Sebastian. The running child had bumped his table, causing the granita to fall on the floor. Glass shattered all over the place. "Ah! Children have so much energy!" he thought.

"I am sorry, sir. I'll get you another granita. May I bring you some towels to dry your pants?" offered the waiter.

"Thank you, that would be great. Although the weather is so hot my pants will be dry soon enough."

Bar 'La Pescheria' was one of the oldest establishments in town. Located in the center of the city, opening on one side to the fish market and on the other to the main square, it was blessed by a steady influx of customers looking for something to eat, refuge from inclement weather, and most of all its core product: one of the best granita on the island. Sebastian had really looked forward to his coffee and almond treat, now mostly splattered on the ground. He checked his backpack to make sure his laptop and phone had not been damaged and noticed a new voicemail had been left.

"Gloria!" he exclaimed pondering for a few moments if a reply was due or not. He then realized that unless he called her back she would have probably jumped on the first flight to Sicily.

He dialed her number breathing deeply and hoping for Gloria's to be too busy to answer.

"Sebastian! Are you ok? Where are you? Talk to me! Have you been kidnapped? I knew it! Don't say anything. Just answer yes or no. I watched all the Sopranos. I know you can't talk right now. Tell me. Did they cut off a finger? Do you still have ears? Your eyes! They took out your eyes! Oh my

God! Claire! Book me a flight to Sicily. And call my security guard. Make sure he meets me at the airport. We are on a rescue mission!"

"Gloria! Please stop! I am fine."

"Are you sure? You can tell me. Don't worry. I won't say anything about your finances. They can torture me. I have it all set up. Passwords. Secret Codes. Change of client ownership. Your secrets are safe with me, and I'll take them to my grave."

"Gloria. I promise. I am ok."

"Sebastian, you cannot possibly be ok! I have charges for rental cars, flight upgrades, bookings at hotels you could never afford. What the hell is going on?"

"My clients may have gone a bit overboard."

"Your clients?"

"Yes. Right now all the expenses are charged directly to my credit card. As soon as the trip is over I'll put the money back in my account."

"Honey, are you ill? I belong to a global network of doctors. I'm pretty sure there is a representative in Sicily. You need serious help!"

"What are you talking about, Gloria? I trust you will take the best financial decisions for my accounts."

"Hon, people with savings or stock have accounts! You don't have accounts anymore. You have more debt than a small country. It will take me years to get you back on your retirement plan!"

"Gloria, I'm not retiring any time soon, and I promise, in a few of weeks all money will be back in your hands."

"I really hope so but I'm really worried. I'll move a few things around to keep you afloat but please come to your senses! Got to go now. Love ya. Bye!"

"Bye Gloria."

Sebastian looked at his freshly served granite and the fragrant brioche on the side but he had lost his appetite. He paied his bill and left without noticing that, behind him, a couple had entered Bar 'La Pescheria'

\* \* \*

"I lost him! He was too fast. When I got out of the church, there was no trace of him. I looked everywhere in the fish market and asked around but nobody had seen him. On my way back to the church, I saw the old woman from inside the church. She was buying flowers for the altar and I asked her if she had seen the child."

"What did she say?" asked John choosing a table overlooking the fish market and offering a chair to Laura.

"She said that she had seen no children. Just angels."

"Angels?"

"Yes. Poor woman. I think she's lost it. Aging is horrible. Makes you think and see things that are not real."

"Laura, that wasn't nice at all! What if what she saw … Or what she thinks she saw, is actually real?" John gestured to a waiter to let him know that the table needed cleaning. A glass with a white and brown granita had been left along with an untouched brioche. "Why would anybody leave anything so delicious behind?" he thought.

"Are you really suggesting she can see angels flying all over town?" Laura picked the menu and started perusing it. Too many choices. "Oh my, I forgot there were so many different kinds of granita! And there it is! Gelsi."

"Gelsi? What's that?"

"They are like blackberries. But blue instead. And enormous! There used to be a gelsi bush in my Sicilian home. I remember spending one summer afternoon picking the most luscious and plump gelsi. Hands and tongue overed with blue juice. And my clothes as well. My mother was livid! My clothes were permanently stained. I was grounded for a long time."

"Good afternoon, welcome to Bar La Pescheria. Would you like something to drink? Today is really hot," offered the waiter.

"Definitely!" answered John. "I read chinotto is something very special in this part of the island. What is it?"

"It looks like coca cola, but it tastes more like a bitter-sweet version of orange juice. I'll bring you a sample so you can have a taste of it."

"Great. Can you also bring us two granitas? One like the one that was left on this table. It looks and smell incredible."

"Almond and coffee? Good choice. We make our own almond milk for the granita. Anything else?"

"Yes, a gelsi granita. Is that a good one?"

"You can bet. This is the season for gelsi. They come directly from the Etna volcano. You will love it."

"Perfect! And two of those brioches, please."

"Sure. I'll be back in a minute." The waiter cleaned up the table Sebastian had left behind.

"I'm impressed!" said Laura.

"For what?" John got closer.

"You ordered like a Sicilian without me saying anything to you."

"Did I? Well, I must admit Francesca, my Travel Concierge helped me. She told me about the chinotto and the brioches. She even showed me a picture of granita INSIDE a brioche!"

"Oh, that we are definitely going to do. I'll show you how to do that properly."

Time slows when emotions and feelings take over. Tales of chinotto's production from orange-like plants, the uniqueness of Sicilian granita, the traditions linked to scooping the inside of a brioche to fill it with granita or the 'skinning' of the outermost, roasted part of the brioche to reveal the softer inside. Two grown up children, rediscovering lightness in life.

"This was so much fun! Time for me to visit Sicilian men's bathrooms. Here is my wallet. I'll ask the waiter to bring us the check and two espressos topped with lemon zest. I'll be back in a minute." John left the table and approached the waiter, who showed him the way to the restrooms and brought two glasses of fresh water and lemon to the table.

Laura opened John's wallet to pay for the check. Among credit cards and Euros, she found a small wallet-size picture of herself smiling at a radiant Lilly.

*I thought we had thrown away everything that reminded us of her*

Overtaken by emotion, Laura put the wallet on the table and started searching for a napkin inside her purse.

"Ehi! Little boy! Stop! Get back right now!" The waiter yelled suddenly.

Laura looked where the wallet had been just a few seconds ago. It was gone.

"Signora! The boy took your wallet! I'll get him right now."

"No!" Laura started chasing the boy. She had recognized him immediately-the boy she had seen inside the church. She elbowed a few people to get closer, but she had a hint as where he was going. As she expected, the boy ran through the fish market and disappeared inside the Church of St. Michael. Laura stopped at the entrance of the church and look up. The champion of all Christians, the Archangel Michael, smiled at her from above. Once again.

The choir from Excelsior had finished its rehearsal. The church was quiet and empty. She searched all over: no trace of the boy. Sitting near a chapel set at the very end of the church, Laura noticed the old woman she had met few hours earlier. She seemed to be sleeping again. But once she got closer, she noticed she was praying, a lava stone rosary in her hands.

"Excuse me madam, have you seen a boy?"

"A boy? No. No boys inside this church."

"I am really sorry to bother you. But I'm pretty sure that a boy came into this church. He stole my wallet."

"No boys here, *signurinedda.* [(7)] . She paused for a few moments, then closed her eyes and recited a few prayers. "However …" she opened her eyes and looked back to Laura. "Angels live all around us."

Laura didn't know what to say. Had the old lady lost her mind? Angels?

"Have you seen any … ehm… 'angel' lately inside this church?"

"All the time, my child. All the time."

"Where?"

"Where they always are. Around us."

Laura lost hope. "Thank you so for your help." She started to leave.

"The one you are looking for, however… that one, you may find him above us."

"Above us…" Laura stood up and looked around and above her. As she walked through the main nave of the church, she saw frescos of Jesus and the apostles, statues of prophets and saints and endless, colorful mosaics of angels led by St. Michael. On her way back to the entrance, Laura noticed one of the jewels of the church, its majestic, golden organ.

"Above us... There must be a way to get the organist up there," she thought, scrutinizing the walls for signs of hidden doors. Behind the baptismal font, Laura noticed something that looked like a wooden cabinet. On a chair nearby, a small basket with a few clothes and a small coke. She opened the cabinet to discover an entrance to a staircase. "It must be this one."

It was dark inside. Laura used the light of her phone to climb the very narrow stairs until she found a small door. She opened it and found herself at the level of the organ which filled almost the entire space, leaving no room for anyone to hide. Not even a small child. She looked up to the ceiling. The angels looked so close she could almost touch them. Far away, up on the dome of the church, the object of the angels' attention, God, blessed his children from above.

*John was correct. The old woman was right... in her own way. Angels are all around and above her. But the one I am looking for is not here.*

She decided to go back to the bar. "John must be looking for me by now." She stopped for a second to look down from the choir's balcony and appreciate the quiet and beauty of the church, just for another moment.

It was then the boy came out of the same hidden door she had just used to get up to the organ level. "How on Earth? Ehi! You! Wait!" She started screaming from above and rushed downstairs.

# CHAPTER LI

### *Church of St. Michael, Acireale, Sicily*

"How did he do that? Where was he hiding? How did I miss him?" Laura could not believe the little boy had been able to deceive her and sneak away that easily. This time, while walking down, she carefully monitored the walls of the staircase. At the half point, Laura noticed something she had missed on her way upstairs. On her right side, a small door had been carved into the wall. She stopped and opened the door.

The space inside was completely dark and she could not feel a light switch on the wall. Something in her pants started vibrating.

"Incoming call from John."

"The Travel Concierge! John!" Laura shouted.

"Where are you? I have been looking for you all over the fish market. Are you ok?"

"Yes. The little child we saw early on stole your wallet. I followed him back to the church. John! You must see this. Please come over!"

"I am not far away. Wait for me."

"There is a wooden built-in nearby the Holy Water fountain. It looks like a large cabinet, but it's a door instead. Come up the stairs. I'm half way up in a small room."

"Be careful. I'm on my way, Laura."

With the Travel Concierge on, Laura was able to cast some light. She walked around until she found the light switch.

Wooden statues painted with bright colors and covered with gold.

Chandeliers of many intricate shapes, incense burners, a wall of giant candles and behind that, an improvised bed made of some old altar clothes and a pillow that looked like it came from one the chairs on the altar. All seemed surreal to Laura, like coming out of a tragic movie. But nothing had prepared her for what she saw next.

The wall behind the improvised bed was covered with pictures of children. No, not all of them. In the middle, a picture of a family. Mum, dad and three little children smiling at the camera. Near that family, the picture she had just held a few minutes earlier. John and Laura from a happier past looking at Lilly.

*Who are these children? Who is the family in the middle? Why did the child steal these pictures?*

Laura felt sick. She turned to the door ready to leave the room when she found the wallet on the floor. Nothing was missing. Except Lilly's picture. She picked it off the wall and put it back in the wallet. Then she found herself on the church's main floor with no memory of how she had gotten downstairs.

The old woman was sitting near the baptismal font, close to the door from which Laura had just come. She seemed to be praying. Her hands held a small basket with clean clothes, some food and a Coke.

"Who's the boy?" whispered Laura sitting nearby the old woman.

"Boys live in homes. With parents and siblings. Only angels live inside a church."

"Where's he from?"

"Many people have crossed the sea. Their homes destroyed. Their lives changed forever. Their families … Gone. Like ashes blown away by the wind." A tear marked her face. "A little angel came through these doors looking for help, rest and refuge. Whoever bore him into this world has disappeared, lost at sea."

"Hoe horrible!" Laura brought her hands to her face and started sobbing.

"I was young once. Beautiful as you are. And married like you to a handsome guy. God never gave us children when we could have taken care of them. And now that I am too old …"

She looked Laura in the eye. "I brought him here. For protection. Nobody knows of him … At least officially. Here he is safe for now. But he needs help I can't give him." She took Laura's hands and squeezed them. "They will find him soon. Maybe you can help him."

"Me? How?" Laura backed away. "What does he need? Food? Money? Clothes?"

"That is for children. Not for angels."

Laura paced a few steps, feeling overwhelmed, angels looking at her from walls and ceilings. She finally sat beside the old woman. "What do angels need, then?"

The old lady's look was intense. "Love. Angels need love."

"Laura!" John called. "There you are! You look terrible. Come outside and get some fresh air. Maybe that will help."

Laura nodded to the old woman and hung on to John, letting him guide her to the bright light that flooded the church's square.

"Come, let's have a seat back at the bar. You need something to drink."

"I need to talk to you, John. I really do."

John started to lead her toward the fish market but Laura suddenly stopped. "Stop! We have got to do something!"

"Laura, I don't understand. You run away chasing a boy and you disappear. I've been looking for you right and left -I even called the police. I finally connect with you and you ask me to run to the church. When I find you, your face is as white as one of the linens spread on the church's altar. And now you're talking about doing something…" John caressed Laura's face.

"Something about what?"

Laura closed her eyes and took a deep breath, then looked at John. "You are right. You need some explanation. Let's go to the bar. We both need something to drink."

\* \* \*

"Fernando! Thank God I found you. Were you sleeping?"

"No, why should I? I was waiting for your daily call to wake me up in the middle of the night. Go on. So I can finally go to bed. Some of us work during the day. What happened?"

"Fernando. You can't possibly be sleeping. It's noon."

"In Italy! Sebastian. It's 4:00 a.m. in Minneapolis."

"Well, time to get up then. As my friend Maarten says, all entrepreneurs wake up early in the morning to get their daily taks done before all normal people get even to work."

"Sebastian!"

"Yes?"

"I am a normal person. I would actually start behaving even more normally if I could sleep a full night."

"Can't you go to bed earlier?"

"Sebastian, please. I am not in the mood. What happened? The Travel Concierges are not working?"

"I don't know. I was walking and all of a sudden I got a crazy sound coming out from the app that links my phone with one of the devices."

"What does the message say?"

"Alert: Device Tracker Activated"

"There you have it."

"What?"

"One of the devices' tracking capability was activated."

"Why would that be?"

"No idea. Maybe one of your clients got lost and the other one was trying to locate her or him? I have a suggestion. Why don't you follow your clients? Isn't that the reason why you are there?"

"What if they recognize me?"

"Well, if they do, say hi and ask for feedback! Do something, but try not to wake me up every night. Good night."

"Fernando?"

"Yes!"

"I think you need to go to a doctor. Since I have left Minneapolis, you've sounded very short tempered on the phone. Maybe your blood pressure is getting too high…"

CHAPTER LI

Click.

"Fernando?"

* * *

"I'm telling you! The boy has lost his entire family and is now living inside the church. No, worse: he is living in a storage room inside a church. We have to do something. We need to call the authorities. Maybe the Embassy."

"Laura, think about it. From what you have told me, the old lady found the boy and hid him in the church. That means that calling the authorities would not be helpful at all. I don't know about Italian laws, but if they work like in the United States, the old lady would be arrested and the boy would be sent back to his home country. Which could lead to his death."

"What can we do then?"

"If the boy has been able to hide in the church, there is one additional person who must be in the know."

"Who?" Laura's eyes were hopeful.

"The priest. Let's go back to the church before it closes for the afternoon Sicilian 'siesta.'"

* * *

Sebastian traced back his steps following the indications provided by his app. He passed Main Square, Bar La Pescheria and the Fish Market. He found himself at the footsteps of a church. The Archangel Michael judging him from above.

# CHAPTER LII

### *Church of St. Michael, Acireale, Sicily*

"Don Gennaro, I am not lying. There is a boy living in the storage room under the staircase leading to the organ. You must know something!" Laura was starting to lose her patience. Why wasn't he listening? Why would he not believe her? "Come with me. I'll show you." Laura started walking out the sacristy, determined to show the priest she was not crazy.

"Signora," Don Gennaro said. "I want you to understand that I am not going to follow you to the storage room."

"Why? Why can't you come with me? I'll demonstrate to you that the boy is actually living under your roof!"

"Think about it. If you are wrong, there is no boy living under the protection of God. That will not make you happy, just angry with me. If the boy does exist … he won't be able to live under the protection of God anymore as I would have to call the authorities. Would that really make you happy? I don't think so. You see, regardless of the choice I make, you will not end up happy. So, I am asking you. What is the point of me following you?"

Laura pondered the options. She looked at John for guidance and she started to talk, when John made a sign to indicate the priest was not done.

"For what I am concerned, there is no boy living in the storage room. The boy does not exist. Period."

"Thank you, Don Gennaro. It was nice talking to you." Laura took John's hand and started walking toward the exit of the church.

"Before you leave, I must tell you that Signora Carmela has been waiting for you nearby the Holy Fountain. Would you please be so kind to stop by her on your way out?"

The old woman was sitting at her usual place: a basket full of bread and water nearby.

"John, will you please wait for me outside?" Laura asked. "I need to talk to her."

"I'll stay here with you. Just in case you'd happen to run away again. There are a couple of men sitting in the church as well. This is not a 'women's only' establishment." John smiled. "I'll light a candle for us. Maybe St. Michael will protect us during our trip in Sicily... and beyond."

"Sure", said Laura. "I'll get back to you in a few."

She walked toward the lady who now had a name: Signora Carmela.

"Signora Carmela," Laura asked. "Did you want to talk to me?"

"Angels are strong, but sometimes they need help."

"I know. But I don't know what to do."

"A few days ago, some bad people came looking for angels who may live in this place. They were not looking to worship the angels, but to take them away. 'This is the house of God!' said Don Gennaro. He told them only God, his son and the Holy Spirit lived in this Holy Place. All people were welcome while the doors of the church were opened."

"He lied?"

"He did not. He never talked about children living inside the church. There is one door on the other side of the altar which leads to the kids' playground. If the door is left open..."

"Everyone is welcome..." said Laura. "Do you know who can help us?"

"When I was young, we used to ask the older people. They always knew what to do. But now I am too old. All the old people are dead ...Or their brains are dead". Signora Carmela took Laura's young hands and held them in hers, warm and marked by years of hard labor. "In any case. You won't get anything from old people. What I would do, is to think like a modern child. There is one thing I have learned from today's children."

"How to sing?"

"I am old. Not senile... yet." Smiled Signora Carmela. "How to Google, my child. I have learned how to Google."

\* \* \*

For just a moment, Sebastian had thought John would come and sit by him. He had built so many convoluted stories on why somebody from the United States would end up in that specific church in Sicily. Luckily for him, John had not stopped. Maybe because he did not want to interrupt his meddling with the phone.

"So that is the story," thought Sebastian. "They found a boy hidden in the church and they are trying to do something." It was impossible not to hear the Laura's conversation with Don Gennaro." At his entering inside the church, he had noticed an old woman sitting in the very last pew and nodding as Don Gennaro was explaining to Laura why her request to follow her to the boy's hiding place made no sense.

Using his tracking device's history, Sebastian found the storage room and saw the pictures on the wall. Now he could understand why Laura was so distraught. He, felt powerless. "But there has to be something I can do," he thought as he was leaving the church. He was the child's age when he last had been in Sicily with his father. The fish market had been always his favorite place. So many new creatures to learn about. So many different people. So many places to hide with his friends...

"Lucia!" Sebastian started searching for his friends' phone number.

"Lucia," he said to her voicemail, "This is Sebastian. I need to talk to you urgently. Please call me back. I am confident you will be very interested in the topic."

# CHAPTER LIII

*Acireale, Sicily*

Laura and John went back to Pensione Mirabella. "Signora Maria, could we have some white wine, please?" Their journey to the little hotel by the sea had been extremely difficult. Laura was inconsolable. She could not fathom leaving the little boy another night alone "inside a damn closet room with nobody to keep him safe and love him. Just mice, dust and God only knows what else."

"Laura, there's not much we can do. Even the priest is trying to ignore the situation just to protect him. He knows the alternatives wouldn't be good at all."

"But there has to be a way to help him. There has to be a place he can go. Why are Italians so heartless?" cried Laura.

"Did I hear you talking about heartless Italians? What happened?" Signora Maria asked bringing a bottle of her best home-made white wine. A quick look at Laura's face told Signora Maria the situation was serious. "Uhff. Let me sit with you for a minute. This heat is killing me. Tell me. What's up?" she said grabbing Laura's hands.

"Today we found a child living inside a church," John said.

"Not inside a church!" Interjected Laura. "In a CLOSET, inside a church. With no bed, no bathroom, no family. NOTHING!"

"I see," said Signora Maria, nodding and pouring wine into three glasses. "Do you think the boy was abandoned or a refugee?"

"We talked to Don Gennaro, the church's priest," said John. "He didn't say anything specific. He actually denied the child even existed."

"A refugee then." Signora Maria gulped her glass all at once like a shot of tequila and filled it with more wine.

"How can you be so sure?" replied Laura.

"If he were an orphan, he could be placed in an Institute. As a refugee… He is nobody. He has no legal status." Signora Maria put her hands on her face, as if stretching her skin up would help her finding a solution. "I can only say that if I were younger, I would probably try to adopt him. All my children are grown up and with the exception of Nico, who works with me, I never see them much around anymore. But I am too old. The Government would never allow it."

"Adopt him? How?" asked Laura.

"Adoptions are complicated in Italy. Too many rules: you are too old, too poor, too gay… Our lawyers make lots of money on adoptions. I need to think about it, kids. Let me go check what my son is doing before he burns down the kitchen."

Laura and John looked at each other. Words were not necessary. They both started typing on their devices.

* * *

"Sebastian, you again? Twice in a day?"

"Fernando! Hi! Where are you?"

"At work. Like any normal person in the middle of the week. Let me guess. You need help."

"Finally you are at work. It was time! Afternoon is almost over. I have a crazy question for you."

"Jesus Sebastian. I don't know why I am even answering! It may be afternoon in Italy but it is just 8:00 a.m. in Minneapolis. What do you need?"

"I need you to hack the devices."

"Excuse me?"

"I need you to hack both Travel Concierges and tamper with their

210

searches."

"Why? Are they broken? Are they giving wrong results?"

"I need you to just trust me. I need you to force the devices to bring up a specific contact information whenever a search is made."

"Are you asking me to overrule Google's algorithm?"

"Don't be silly. Nobody can do that...Can you?"

"Nobody can? Of course I can. I built those stupid apps based on your designs! Have you forgotten? No need to hack Google's algorithm. Just the devices. "

"Well, there you have it. I'm sending you the information I need you to show on the top section of every search."

"What kind of contact am I going to 'suggest' to your clients? Nothing illegal, I hope."

"Perfectly legal. The contact information is a law office."

"A legal office? Are you in trouble? Why do you need a lawyer?"

"Not a lawyer. An adoption lawyer. Thank you, Fernando!"

Click.

"Sebastian?" *Why do I continue answering his calls?*

# PART XI

*An angel leaves his nest*

# CHAPTER LIV

*Pensione Mirabella, Acireale, Sicily*

The view of the bay was incredible: small boats slowly sailing crossing the waters; seagulls suspended in the air; children playing on the sandy beach below. From his balcony, John wondered at how beautiful and serene life could be. Just a day earlier, he had thought that his bond with Laura had been rekindled. They were talking and laughing together like they had before Lilly. But that brief moment had been crushed by the discovery of a young boy living alone and in dire conditions inside a church.

Silence and awkwardness had returned. And Laura's restless nightly dreams were anticipating another challenging day. John had a choice. Either silently go along with Laura's mood for the rest of the trip and risk all that he had fought for, or react and do something about it. A gentle breeze flowed from the Etna volcano and a few clouds dotted the sky. Maybe the day would not be as hot as usual. From high above John could hear children's laughter becoming louder and louder. The sound of a call coming from somewhere unknown. He had made his decision.

John went back inside and called the Concierge. Signora Maria answered and talked before he could even open his mouth. "Your breakfast is on its way," she said and hung up.

"She really knows her customers," thought John. He sat on the bed and stroked Laura's hair. Laura opened her eyes, still red from crying all night long.

"I want you to show me your nest. Take me to your family spot on the seashore."

Laura looked at him, puzzled at first. But she finally nodded and went to the bathroom. John wondered if his decision had been the right one and if he should have just waited for her to wake up and decide how to spend the day. When he heard the sound of the shower running, he knew Laura was trying to react and move forward one small step at the time. He had made the right choice.

A knock at the door announced that breakfast was ready. And as always, Signora Maria's treatment had been exceptional. Scrambled eggs, smoked salmon, fresh yogurt topped with honey and strawberries, the softest brioches John had ever seen and hot espressos sprinkled with lemon zest.

"What is this smell?" asked Laura just coming out of the shower. She looked at the spread of food and turned to John. "Signora Maria really thinks that all problems and pains can be treated with food ... I don't think that's possible but this food really helps a lot." She smiled at John, "You better get ready for a long walk." John replied with a smile and went to take a shower.

\* \* \*

"Incoming call from Maarten."

"Oh no! Too early in the morning. Does that guy not sleep at night?"

"Sebastian! How are you?"

"I am great. Where are you today?"

"Lord only knows. Leave it to my assistant. I am in a hotel filing for a patent. The only thing I can see is sea all around me."

"Must be a nice place your assistant sent you to."

"Paper, Sebastian. A sea of paper. Trying hard to get to my first billion. Maybe this patent will do it."

"You mean Million?"

"Billion. With the B. I passed the Million mark years ago, Sebastian. Now. Seriously. I just got off the phone with your friend Gloria. According to her, if your clients continue spending at current rate, by the time you'll be back to Minnesota, your 401K will be worth 4 OR 1 K." Maarten started laughing.

"Am I supposed to laugh?"

"Not at all! But you must admit it would make it for a great joke!"

"Sure. If I don't make it as an entrepreneur, I'll try a career as a stand-up comic."

"You are a trooper!" Maarten continued laughing "You can still laugh as you fall into financial ruin! I think you are getting it!"

"What?"

"The bug, Sebastian, the bug. Listen, I need to finish this filing before the competition does. Try to connect with your clients and get them to spend less or at least to give you their approval to charge their credit cards. Ciao.

# CHAPTER LV

*"Le Chiazzette", Acireale, Sicily*

T here was no parking available for where they were going, so they left the car near the church of Saint Michele. "Just one John, I promise." Laura went into the church and lit a candle. "Dear St. Michael, please protect the soul and life of the little boy. Keep him safe and give him guidance." A tear streaked her face as she set the candle in a container full of sand. She looked at the statue of St. Michael. So strong. A fearless leader. A protector of all the church's souls.

Laura suddenly felt like she was not alone. "Somebody is looking at me." She looked around but saw nobody. Not even Donna Carmela. She finally made the sign of the cross and knelt before leaving the church. As she turned around, she felt the warm sun on her face again. Not as hot as in the previous days. Just pure light. Enfolding and reassuring.

"Let's go!" she said to John.

They walked through old streets. Laura talked about famous families who once used lead the town. She told John everything she remembered. "In Sicily, the best buildings used to have stores on the ground floors. The store owners paid a rent to the owners of the building. The richer the store, the higher the status of the owner. Majestic and beautiful iron gates would lead the guests to the gardens, set in the middle of the building. From the gardens, where carriages and horses would stay, marble staircases would take you to splendid living rooms, ballrooms and music rooms. The family members would sleep on the next floor, and on the top floor- hottest in

216

summer and coldest in winter- would live an army of butlers, nurses, cooks, seamstresses and cleaning crews. Each palace was its own world. With its rules and lords."

"It must have been an amazing time!"

"Only if you were a member of the aristocracy, honey," Laura smiled.

They walked on ancient roads made of lava stone. "There is plenty of lava in a land shaped by a volcano. It is strong but very dangerous. When it rains, it gets very slippery."

"I guess I'll make sure not to wear heels during rainy season!" smiled John.

The road led them through an arch. "Built to allow people to still use the road once trains started running, it was a good thought to plan a train line above the road. The old way of life continued until..."

"Until what?" said John.

They arrived at the end of the tunnel where a small guard rail marked the end of the old road. "Until highways. This part of the island is very narrow. A high cliff leading to the sea marks east and the volcano towers on the last from the west. Not much terrain is left for North/South traffic. This is going to be fun!"

John felt like playing Frogger. The only difference was... He and Laura were the frogs trying not to get killed by maniac car drivers. It took some patience, luck and very fast legs. But eventually they reached the other side of the highway.

"How do Sicilians do that every day?"

"We don't. We leave it to the tourists. But you will really love what's next. Come."

Laura led John to an even older road. The slabs of lava stone were marked by thousands of carriages and innumerable feet. Part of the road was set in large, rectangular, steps slowly sloping downhill. Part was flat to allow the passage of horses, donkeys and carriages. Left and right small arches once hosted shops and tool makers.

"The larger steps resemble a small square or *Piazza*, as we call it in Italian," Laura started. "In dialect, a *Piazza* is called *Chiazza*. As this road is made of steps and many small piazzas, the name 'Chiazzette' seems just appropriate."

A little, simple church carved in the rock on the right side. On the left side, the steps led downhill. John looked at was in front of him.

"This is spectacular!"

"Just one of the best views of the Mediterranean sea." Laura smiled. "Ancient Greeks founded the first city a few miles south. Old writings state the original city was large and beautiful, but it was completely destroyed by a lava fall. The refugees built a new city, but this time they chose higher ground."

"Higher? This must be…"

"An almost perfectly vertical cliff of about 700 feet above the sea. Technically, we are standing on a terrace carved on the African continental platform. Down there, where the sea waves crush with the rocks and a few houses, churches and storage buildings make up the old port, is the European platform."

"Breathtaking," John whispered.

"It is. And imagine how beautiful this road must have been in the past." Laura led John down the road. "Carriages and flocks of people once filled with sounds, merchandise and sweat the cobblestone road that took from the city all the way down to the port. But now, only a handful of tourists take the time to walk up and down the stairs under an iron-hot sun."

They walked slowly. A few clouds protected them from the heat. "Just another perfect day" thought John.

They talked about all the endemic plants and animals that lived just on the cliff, the color and features of which you could only find in that part of the world. Laura taught John how to interpret the different varieties of lava rocks: "Red ones are full of iron. Light ones packed with gas when they came out of the volcano via explosions. Yellow rocks smell like sulfur. My dad was very passionate about his land and shared everything he knew. Even after we moved to the united States…" She suddenly stopped.

"Are you ok Laura?"

"I've been having the feeling that somebody is following us since we left the church."

They looked around but didn't see anybody, except an older man riding a mule uphill.

"When I was little, there used to still be many people on donkeys going up and down this road. And shepherds leading large herds of sheep and goats. John, I wish you'd been here. It was so much fun."

"I am sure it was. Now, let's get to the shore. I want to get to the beach," said John.

"Beach? Sure. But I don't think this is the kind of beach you are used to." Laura laughed.

At the end of the steps, a small kiosk welcomed thirsty visitors with fresh beverages and small sandwiches. "Time for a soda," said Laura.

"Nice! Coke? Sprite?"

"Don't be silly! A Sicilian soda is made of ice-cold sparkling water and lemon or orange juice squeezed on the spot from real fruits. And we add a pinch of salt too."

"Always something to learn! Can't wait to try one."

Sodas in hand, Laura and John walked to the "beach."

"This is all pebbles! Where is the sand?" asked John.

"The only sandy spot around here is where Pensione Mirabella is-like a small island surrounded by lava and tectonic platforms. This pebble beach, instead, was created by centuries of erosion and water activity. The closer you get to the water, the smaller the pebbles." Laura pointed north and south of the pebble beach. "However, as you can see, a few feet from here, rocks rule again." She winked at John. "Let's get moving toward the rocks. Fewer people."

"Sure. But let's not go too far. The clouds are getting thicker. I want to be able to get back to the car in case it starts raining."

Laura took off her shoes and started hopping from one pebble to the other one. She chose the larger and more stable ones: easier to keep her balance. She turned around and saw that John was trying to copy her moves. But stumbling a few times. "Always fall on your butt!" laughed Laura. "It hurts less".

"Now I know how Sicilians keep staying fit: walking a lot and hopping on pebbles!"

"I also read that walking on rocks with your bare feet stimulates your brain. It's good for your synapses."

"My synapses are screaming that the rocks are hot!"

Laura laughed and sped up.

When they arrived at the end of the beach, large, massive rocks, tumbled from the cliff all the way to the sea, created dozens of small, private enclosures. Laura put her running shoes back on and advised John to do the same. "These rocks are like obsidian. You can cut your feet easily if you don't know what you are doing."

Laura finally found what she was looking for. A large rock, flat on top. From there she could see the beach for miles on both sides. The cliff grew tall on her back. In front of them the immensity of the Ionian sea. She started undressing.

"What are you doing?" said John. "We don't have swimming suits!"

"We are going to swim as Sicilian children used to do. We called it "all'angelina"

"Al what?"

"Naked like the angels. Follow me!"

She slowly walked into the sea. "Walk slowly and only on black rocks or brown algae."

"So many rules in Sicily! What happens if I walk on the green ones?"

"You'll fall."

"And I guess not having a swimming suit won't help, right?"

"Definitely not!" Laura laughed.

John took off his clothes and hopped on a few rocks until he got to the shore. "Oh my God! It's freezing!" He tried not to fall. "I thought the water in the Mediterranean Sea would be warm this time of the year"

"It would be. If it wasn't for the fresh water."

"But this is salt water. I can taste it!"

"It is, but fresh water runs from the volcano down to the seashore. An old legend states that the original city was built near a large river. The lava fall that destroyed the city, also covered the river. There are countless fresh water springs all over the coast. That's why these waters are so... refreshing!"

220

Laura jumped in the sea and John followed. The water warmed around them as they swam away from the coast.

John finally reached Laura. "I love you."

"I love you too," she replied and kissed him. "I wish this moment would never end."

"Me too," replied John playing with her hair.

"If only…" she started. "Wait a minute… Look at that boy over there … That is … Yes. That is the boy from the church! I knew somebody was following us. Come! We need to talk to him."

They quickly swam back to the shore and got dressed. "He's running away" said John.

"He can't run fast on these rocks. And I have more practice. I'll get him. Catch up with me at the bottom of the stairs."

"Laura! Wait!"

But it was too late. Laura had a target. And that target was running away from her.

# CHAPTER LVI

*"Le Chiazzette", Acireale, Sicily*

"The little Tasmanian devil! He was too fast. I lost him again." John found Laura trying to catch her breath.

"Do you really think he was following us?"

"Yes, I am sure, John. He must be really good at hiding."

"Who knows what he has gone through in his life? Listen, we better start getting back uphill. The clouds are getting thicker and I wouldn't want to get surprised by a storm on a medieval staircase carved into a cliff. Even though the view is spectacular."

"You're right. Let's get back to the car. Maybe we can find him inside St. Michael. I have so many questions."

As John and Laura climbed the stairs, the sky slowly darkened. Laura turned toward the sea. "Look at the sea, John"

"Incredible! It's like steam rising up from the sea."

"This is how the clouds *feed*. The gather their moisture from the sea." Laura closed her eyes and breathed in deeply. "And feel the breeze."

"It's coming from the sea."

"If it comes from the sea hang your hoe on the wall and start cooking"

"What does that mean?" asked John.

"We better hurry. It's going to rain. And a lot!"

They were not even half way when the drops started falling. The fresh water was nice, at first. A refreshing balm for hot, sweaty climbers. But the rain soon thickened and thunder grew louder.

"We need to get to the top as soon as possible. In a few minutes these lava stone steps are going to be as slippery as if they were covered with olive oil." Said Laura

"I wish we had some warm bread then."

"What are you talking about, John?"

"Bruschetta?"

"Oh my God! You are becoming Sicilian. Always thinking about food! And by the way..."

"What?"

"That was a really good one." Laura looked around for a safe place. "There they are. The arches! We'll find refuge there."

"Should we go on and get to St. Michael?"

"Too far away. This cliff will soon be flooded with water running down from the city."

Only then John noticed that more and more water was coming down uphill. It was either from the highway above or the city itself, and it was not a good thing. They ran to the safety of what used to be an old warehouse. It wasn't big, but at least provided some protection.

"Well, at least Signora Maria will be happy. She has been complaining about the heat and dry conditions since we got here," said John.

"I wish we had enough time to get to the church. I wonder where the boy is right now... John, do you think we could do something for him?"

"Like?"

"I don't know. Maybe refer him to a foster home or connect with the U.S Consulate to get him refugee status."

"I'm not sure ..."

"Incoming call from Mrs. Lucia Aliberti," announced Francesca, the Travel Concierge.

"Did you?" Asked Laura.

"What can I say? I am not completely stone-hearted. I did some research and her name came up on top. Mrs. Aliberti lives downtown and looks like she has a great reputation about these kind of things."

"What things, John?"

"Well…you know…adoptions?"

Laura looked at John for a minute. She had no words to express her feelings. She hugged him and kissed him.

"I knew the trip would make me a winner" she softly said.

"Your trip to Sicily?"

"No. Vegas. The place we met. I won the jackpot."

"If I didn't have a call to take…" John quickly kissed Laura and answered the call "Mrs. Aliberti, good afternoon. Thank you so much for calling me back. Did you receive my email with information? Will you be able to help us?"

Laura walked closer to the archway leading to the ancient steps. This is what she had looked for. This is what they both needed. A new opportunity.

The rain was falling hard and wild, the sky pitch black when it had just been sunny and clear. A lightning show streaked before them. Thunder boomed. A sudden wind came up. Laura turned to find John typing on his device. "How did it go? Can she help us?"

"The connection was very unreliable. We are planning to meet tomorrow morning at her office downtown."

"Thank you John. I am so … Surprised and proud of you!"

"Why? Am I so predictable? Come closer. Where were we?"

"You dirty, Scandinavian rascal…" Laura got closer, then suddenly stopped. "Wait a minute. Can you hear that?"

John came closer to the archway. "It sounds like… Somebody crying?"

"Or screaming, maybe. I didn't notice it earlier- the thunder was horribly loud but now the storm is moving away…"

"I think it comes from the chapel on top of the Chiazzette! Somebody might be hurt. Hold my hand Laura, the water rushing down from the highway is quite high. I don't want you to fall."

The cry got lauder as they approached the small church. "It sounds like a child's cry. John! Do you think…"

"Maybe," said John, fighting to keep his balance against the running water.

They finally arrived at the steps of the church. Carved into the cliff itself, the construction was a few steps higher than the ground, safe from sudden water. Laura and John entered the main chapel. "Behind the altar!" Laura whispered.

John nodded and signaled to slowly approach from the opposite side. The only way to keep the boy from running was coming from both sides.

Step by step they got closer. Not a whisper. Just the boy sobbing and the sound of thunder. When they finally got behind the altar, John signaled to Laura that it was time. "Little boy, I am here to help you," said John.

The boy looked up and saw John's silhouette in the dim light of votive candles. Scared, he ran the opposite way, bumping into Laura's arms. "I am here for you, little boy. Don't worry," said Laura.

The boy tried to run again but John quickly came held him firmly. The boy screamed and cried, kicking and trying to escape.

"Non piangere, little one. Don't cry, we are here for you," Laura started to cry.

"Lasciami andare! Let me go! Leave me alone!"

"We are here for you. Can you understand me?"

The boy looked at Laura and nodded.

"We don't want to hurt you. We just want to stay with you while the storm passes by," said John. "We are scared too. Maybe you can help us find our way home?"

The boy looked at them, then outside. The storm was still raging. And water was running strong at the base of the church.

"Ok. I'll stay with you until the end of the storm." said the boy.

"Will you hold me?" said Laura. "I am really scared."

The boy hugged Laura. "It's going to be ok."

John checked his device, hoping it was waterproof. "Ms. Aliberti? This is John. We need your help, if possible."

The storm finally passed and the running water quickly subsided. The boy was now sleeping peacefully in Laura's hands while John's device rang.

"Ms. Aliberti? Yes, we are still inside the church. We have the boy. He is sleeping. We'll be up to the highway in a few minutes. Laura, Ms. Aliberti is up the street, waiting for us."

"Let me wake him up," Laura patted gently the boy on his shoulder. "Hello sleepy. Will you get us to your home? We have a car."

The boy nodded and stood up. John picked him up "This way you won't get wet more than you are not already. Still a lot of water flowing down from the highway."

The three of them walked up the stone steps in ankle-deep running water. A smiling figure was waited for them at the end of the stairway. "Nice meeting you in person, John and Laura. I am Lucia Aliberti. Where are we going?"

Laura looked at the boy and smiled. "We are going to the boy's home. The church of St. Michael."

# CHAPTER LVII

*Church of St. Michael, Acireale, Sicily*

"Sir, I am telling you. There is no boy living in this church. I don't understand why you would come back and bring a lawyer with you. Can you remind me your name?"

"Lucia Aliberti, Don Gennaro. I am an adoption lawyer.

"Don Gennaro, please, let us help you," said John. "I know the boy does not live in the church. But maybe he stops by now and then? Do you know how we could find his family?"

"I don't think you understand me, sir. There is no boy. There is no family."

"Don Gennaro!" the scared face of Signora Carmela suddenly appeared inside the sacristy. "Don Gennaro, they are here!"

"Who, Signora Carmela?"

"The police!" she whispered. "The choir director is entertaining them, introducing them to all the choir members and asking questions. But they will soon be here. What are we going to do?"

"The same thing we do every day at this time of the day," answered Don Gennaro. "We prepare for mass."

"But nobody is here," replied Signora Carmela.

"I see four people in this room and a full choir ready to sing. I would say that is plenty. Now, if you will all excuse me." He looked at John and Lucia. "I need to get ready for mass. Should you two decide to *prepare* as well, you would find a few useful items inside the cupboard set nearby the front door. The items may be more fit to ... *a younger person...* But they should work."

227

Lucia and John, puzzled, looked at each other.

"Also, at the time of the homily, I usually invite the military to come to the altar before anybody else. I do realize that sometimes people have more important matters to take care of and can't wait for the military people to be done. So please, I'll totally understand you having to leave while I take first care of them."

No additional words were needed. Don Gennaro retreated into his dressing room. Donna Carmela, tears in her eyes, took their hands with her trembling ones and kissed them. "Save him," she whispered. She took a candle and lit it.

John and Lucia watched Signora Carmela leave the sacristy and walk to the altar to light a candle. They looked at each other. They had a plan.

# CHAPTER LVIII

*Church of St. Michael, Acireale, Sicily*

The boy let Laura enter his home. He showed her his handful of possessions: a few clothes items, a small pillow, an altar cloth he used as a blanket, a few crayons and dozens of pictures of children attached to a wall. "My friends," he said. "They are all my friends!" In the middle of all of his friends, the boy had a picture of himself held by a couple. Two other children, a younger boy and a tall girl, smiled at their side. "Family," said the child.

Laura held her tears and forced herself to display a big smile. She sat on the floor and asked: "Your family is beautiful! Where do they live?"

The boy picked a red crayon and marked something on the wall. "Land," he said. "Danger." He then picked a blue crayon and drew all around the land. "Sea. Blue as the sky." He put down his blue crayon and picked a yellow one. "Boat. Lots of people."

"John was correct. He is a refugee," thought Laura. "Where is your family?" asked Laura.

"Bang!" The boy mimicked an explosion with his hands. He then picked his family's picture and put it in the middle of the blue area he had just drawn. "Sea," he said.

Laura could not stop her tears anymore. She offered her hand to the boy and he hesitantly took it. The two looked at each other. A choir started singing down below.

*Panis Angelicus Fit Panis Ominum*

"What is your name?" asked Laura. The boy looked at her but did not answer. Laura then remembered what Donna Carmela had said "Only angels live inside a church."

*Dat panis coelicus figuris terminum*

"Can I call you Angelo?" The boy smiled and nodded. Laura got closer.

*O res mirabilis, Manducat Dominum*

"John and I will never be able to be as good as your family but... Would you like to have a family again?"

*Pauper pauper servus et humilis, Pauper pauper servus et humilis*

The boy looked at the wall, all his friends, smiling at him. He then looked at the picture of his family. He blew a kiss to his hand and placed it on the picture.

*Panis Angelicus Fit Panis Ominum*

He looked at Laura and nodded. Then got closer and hugged her.

*Dat panis coelicus figuris terminum*

They both started crying.

*O res mirabilis, Manducat Dominum*

"What about picking up your family and your friends? I'll take you to my home," Laura said. The boy started picking up his treasures. "I'll never forget this moment," she thought, looking at the picture of the boy's family. "And he never will either. But I promise he'll have everything you ever wished for him... And more."

*Pauper pauper servus et humilis, Pauper pauper servus et humilis*

...

John and Lucia sat quietly in the church: first row at the left side of the altar. The two policemen were still at their place guarding the entrance of the church. Behind the altar were the Excelsior choir and Andrew, its Director. Signora Carmela was sitting in her usual place nearby the entrance of the church, in the last row of seats.

"What are we going to do?" said Lucia. "The policemen are guarding the exit. We'll never be able to leave the church".

"What about the gardens? Don Gennaro once mentioned there's a door leading to the children's playground. From there..."

"I am quite confident they already thought about that. They probably have another team guarding the exit."

The choir sang a touching melody and at the end of the song Don Gennaro came out of the sacristy. He looked at the two policemen guarding the entrance of the church, then nodded to the choir. At the signal, the choir started singing again. Don Gennaro walked toward Lucia and John, "Make sure you bring offerings to the altar." Then he pointed to Donna Carmela, sitting at the end of the church.

"I am not sure what to do," John told Lucia.

"Don't worry. It really was a message to go and ask Donna Carmela. Let's sit here until the Offertory. I am sure he is going to give us another sign."

John checked his device. No messages from Laura. But that didn't mean he could not send a message to her. "Troubles inside the church. Remain where you are until I come. Be ready to leave as soon as I send you a signal." He really hoped Laura would receive the message. He sighted with relief when he received the reply back, "We'll be ready."

Don Gennaro performed all his duties as if nothing special was happening. The fact that two policemen were guarding the entrance to his church, or that some people were trying to smuggle an *apparently living inside the church* boy did not affect his performance. He dedicated his homily to all refugees who had to leave their homes to find safety and refuge away from their homelands: in lands where they were mostly not welcomed, if not harassed and taken advantage of. At the end of the homily, he nodded to Lucia and John.

"Show time!" said Lucia.

They kneeled in front of the altar and walked to the back of the church where Donna Carmela was waiting for them with wine and bread to be blessed. "Please give him my golden chain. This is the only precious thing I have." She put the chain in Lucia's hands, "I hope he will remember me. I loved him so much," said Signora Carmela trying to keep back her tears.

John and Lucia walked back to the altar. Don Gennaro looked at the policemen. They looked like two lions waiting to jump to action as soon as mass was over. "The Lamb of God! Offered in sacrifice for all of us!" He looked at the policemen in the eyes. Then he moved his attention to John and Lucia, "And blessed are the souls of these two pilgrims who will bring joy to another land! My children, bring me the rug laid in St. Michal's Chapel. Let me bless it. May this gift from our community to your mission help healing he who comes with you."

John and Lucia looked at each other trying to make sense of Don Gennaro's words. And for a moment Don Gennaro thought his plan would not work. But Signora Carmela had received the message. She rushed to the chapel of St. Michael and rolled the rug at the base of its altar. It was large and heavy but John came quickly to her rescue and lifted it. He brought the rug to the main altar where Don Gennaro blessed it.

"May the two of you help shield the soul of the less fortunate. Your journey will be treacherous and challenging. May your faith in God and your love for the 'angel' guide your path."

Lucia and John kneeled again in front of the altar.

"I got it!" whispered John.

"Let's get this done," replied Lucia. They walked back to the entrance of the church, but from opposite sides. Lucia stopped by the policemen while John sneaked inside the wardrobe behind the fountain with the Holy water.

Donna Carmela walked down the aisle, got the communion cup and brought the Host and wine to the policemen standing at the church's doors. She stopped in front of them and started mumbling a few words in Latin. The two policemen, in respect to the older lady, bent down, waiting for what seemed to them some kind of "blessing" to be over. Lucia positioned herself nearby Donna Carmela, her hands joined in prayer.

Meanwhile the Minnesotan choir started walking from the altar to the entrance of the church. Tenors and altos on one side, sopranos and bass on the other. Dressed in white, they looked like giant, singing wings. The two groups met behind the policemen.

Donna Carmela gave the Host to the policemen, Lucia the wine. The choir, then walked back to the altar to receive communion from Don Gennaro and positioned themselves behind the altar.

"This was the craziest mass I've ever attended," said one policeman. "Let's get back in position," replied the other one. As they returned to the entrance of the church, they noticed John carrying a rug to his car. And two women. One sitting at the driver's seat and the other one at the passenger's side.

"Can you believe they had the priest blessing a rug? A rug! Like there are no other rugs in the world."

"Well, the priest said it was the rug of St. Michael's chapel. Maybe it has some value... But still... A rug is a rug! You're right ... By the way, did you notice that there were two women getting into the car? I thought the missioners were just two people."

"Nah! Look at the altar. One of the sopranos is missing. They are probably giving her a lift."

\* \* \*

Once mass was over, Don Gennaro went back to the sacristy while the choir remained at the altar to rehearse some more. "Don Gennaro, we need to talk to you," said one of the policemen, entering the sacristy.

"How can I help you?"

"I am sure it was just a misunderstanding, but some people have come to the police office complaining, once again, that a refugee child is living under your roof."

"A refugee child? I thought we already had this conversation. "

"Yes, indeed. I am sure you won't mind if we just look around once again for a few minutes. You know, just to be able to let concerned citizens know that we were here and checked everywhere. Not that I am expecting to find anything..."

"Of course," replied puzzled Don Gennaro. "Please, do as you feel necessary."

At that very moment Signora Carmela appeared.

"Don Gennaro, I have cleaned the altar and all around it. That messy choir of angels is gone. NONE of them is left. EVERYTHING is clean and as it is supposed to be. Do you mind if I go home? The rain must have affected my joints, and I'm hurting everywhere."

"Of course Donna Carmela, thank you so much for your help. Lord only knows how much help we all need. Spiritually and physically. I'll see you tomorrow, then."

"Good night, Don Gennaro." Donna Carmela held Don Gennaro's hands and kissed them, said goodbye to the policemen and left the church by the door leading to the gardens. As she passed the playground, she suddenly stopped. For just a moment, she thought she saw an eight-year-old child sitting on top of a slide smiling at her. His young, bright eyes full of hope and dreams.

That night, walking slowly, Donna Carmela took the longest way back home. She prayed in silence: her olive wood rosary clasped in her hands. Each street a prayer, each crossing a Requiem Aeternam, each cobblestone a caring thought for a soul lost.

Before starting the "Luminous", the final section of the Rosary, she stopped and touched her neck, reaching for a gold necklace and started crying. As she prayed for a lost boy on his way to a new life, tears of joy and relief touched every cobblestone she walked on.

# PART XII

*A family on the mending and a family on the run*

# CHAPTER LIX

### *Pensione Mirabella, Acireale, Sicily*

"Gesu', Giuseppe e Maria! Nico! Bring me something to eat. Bedda Matri! (Mother Mary!) This poor boy is dying from starvation!" Signora Maria raised her hands to the sky and motioned her son to hurry. "Where did you find him? Who is he?" She whispered to John and Laura. "No! No! Don't say anything. Better this way."

She looked at them. Laura and John exhausted. The boy looked like he'd come from a third-world place she'd only seen on TV. And the girl with them... Signora Maria winked at her. "Follow me. I'll get you to a more private room."

The group followed Signora Maria to her own living room. Nico brought fresh bread with olive oil, cheeses, meats and a few glasses of water. "You must be very happy, Signora Maria," said John trying to break the ice. "Today we finally had some rain. Your plants and vines must have enjoyed it."

"Rain? You call that disaster rain? It was a BOMB! A real BOMB of water! A cataclysm like no other. It was like the sky opened and the entire ocean of the heavens fell over Sicily. Hopefully tomorrow will be sunny again! Sit. Sit. I'll bring dinner." Signora Maria left the group.

"What should we do, Lucia?" asked John, wondering why everything in Sicily had to be dramatic. First was the "deadly" heat. Now the "cataclysmic" rains. He broke some bread and improvised a small sandwich for the boy.

"We must be very careful to keep the boy out of sight for the time being. I need to make a few calls to some of my colleagues tomorrow morning.

Then I'll connect with you." Lucia said.

"Our flight leaves in two days." Laura interjected. "Should we call the Embassy in Rome and ask for refugee status for the boy?" asked Laura.

"I am sorry. But your new Administration has restricted every opportunity to apply for such an option. Call the Embassy and you will not see the boy for a very long time. Whatever you may think you want to do, please do NOT connect with the Embassy right now. Just keep a low profile for the next 48 hours. I'll call you tomorrow with a plan." Lucia stood up and whispered something to Signora Maria who looked back at John, Laura and the boy, and clasped her hands together. Signora Maria replied something John and Laura could not hear, then left the room.

The boy quietly finished his sandwich, his eyes looking at everything going on around him. He looked at John and asked, "More?"

"Of course." John made him another sandwich and gave it to him. He smiled and caressed his hair. "We'll take care of you. All right?" The boy smiled.

Lucia came back to the table. "I talked to Signora Maria. She now knows a few details but not everything. She also understands that I am a lawyer and that I am trying to help you."

"Would you like to have dinner with us? Please stay," said Laura.

"Thank you for the offer, but I need to study this case and figure out how we can get this boy to the United States in the next 48 hours. You have my phone number. Call me any time." She kissed the boy's head and left.

John took his device and started dialing.

"Who are you calling?" asked Laura.

"The Embassy."

"Why? She just told you not to do that!"

"I know. But I am sure she was wrong. There is no way this boy is staying behind." John left the table and started talking with the Embassy representative.

Laura looked at the boy and smiled. She took her device from her purse. A business card was still tucked in the protective cover. She typed the phone number and wrote a text message. "Dear Ms. Valucelli, this is Laura. I need

239

your help." Laura immediately regretted sending it. "What was I thinking? Like she would reply to a regular person like me. She'll probably laugh," she thought. Then her phone rang. And no one was laughing.

\* \* \*

"Sebastiano! Thank God I found you. I need to talk to you in person right now."

"Lucia! How are you? For some reason, the fact that you are using my Italian name does not sound like a good thing."

"Absolutely not. Are you in your room?"

"Yes. But... How do you know..."

"I know more than you think, Sebastiano. You have no idea what I went through today. I am coming to your room. Stay where you are and wait for me."

\* \* \*

"Mum, dad, I hope you can hear me. These people are nice. They say that they can help me and that I can join their family. I hope you are ok with that. Please keep an eye to my teacher. I wonder how she is now. I wish I had time to say goodbye." Angelo thought holding his new gold chain. "She always sat near the fountain with the Holy Water and sometimes slept there at night. Maybe she did not have a home as well. I usually would come out of my home to keep her company while she slept. Now I won't be able to do that anymore. I wonder if she is sleeping inside the school. Maybe she is alone right now. Maybe she is scared. I'll pray for her tonight."

# CHAPTER LX

### Pensione Mirabella, Acireale, Sicily

"Lucia, how nice to see you again. I can't believe you are at Pensione Mirabella as well," said Sebastian opening his door.

"Sebastian! Do you even know what I just did?"

"No. Not really. Would you like something to drink? I have fantastic wine..."

"Stop right now! I just helped smuggle a boy!"

"Wow! You're lucky we are in Italy. This would be quite illegal in the United States..."

"It IS illegal to smuggle a boy under the police's nose in Italy as well! I could lose my license and get thrown into a jail!"

"Why did you do it then?"

"You really ARE amazing! I did it because you told me to help your clients! And I wanted to help you."

"But I am not the one who asked you to kidnap a boy..."

"Smuggle! Not kidnap. And open that bottle, instead of talking. Will you?"

"Sure. Man, you are quite uptight. So, tell me. What are you going to do now?" Sebastian, offered a glass of wine.

"Me?" Lucia gulped down the full glass. "WE! Honey. We are in this together."

"Well, if that makes you feel better... What are WE going to do?"

"I don't know. We need to figure out a way to get that boy through U.S. Immigration. And we only have 48 hours." Lucia started pacing around the hotel room. "If only there was a way to stop John and Laura from doing something very stupid like calling the Embassy of the United States…"

"Ah! That is easy." Sebastian walked toward a small desk.

"Easy?" Laura followed him. "How?"

"I just have to switch on my computer, connect to the network and lock their devices."

"Can you do that?"

"Sure! Look. Connection established. I just have to access their devices and there you have it. As easy as 1… 2… Oh. Oh"

"What?"

"Too late."

"You can't lock the devices?"

"That I can do but … John called the Embassy a few minutes ago."

"Why can't you men listen? Ever!? I told him not to call the Embassy," said Lucia, now talking with both hands and tongue as only Italians can do. "And what does he do? He calls the Embassy!"

"Lucia, why is that so bad? The Embassy could be very understanding. Maybe they have a solution…"

"Understanding? A solution? You are as naïve as a kindergartener! By now Immigration and Customs has profiled both of them. As soon as they get to the border they'll be questioned and the boy will be sent back home. Regardless of what paper we are going to get ready for him in the next 48 hours!"

"All right. Calm down. It is still not the end of the world. If the boy is sent back to Sicily, we can have Nico pick him up and he can stay with Signora Maria until we figure out his paperwork," Sebastian said.

Overtaken by the tension of the events she had gone through of the past few hours, Lucia started to shiver. Tears filled her eyes.

"Lucia, I know this would not be the best option for the boy. Maybe I could join him on his travel back to Sicily, if you help me with the paperwork?"

"You don't understand." Lucia tried to regain control and master a few words without trembling. "Sicily is not the boy's home."

"Of course it is. He was found here. Where would he go?"

"He is not Sicilian. He is not Italian. He is a refugee. I don't know his home country, but whatever it is, his parents tried to get out and take him along."

Sebastian finally understood the complex and brutal reality of the situation. "There is no way they would send him back there. Would they?"

"Yes, they would!" Lucia walked outside to the balcony overlooking the beach. "The boy will be sent back to the country he was trying to escape. But this time he'll be alone. His parents won't be with him. He will die!"

Sebastian walked toward Lucia. "No. He is not. We still have time. Let me make a call"

He walked to the balcony and dialed a number on his phone. "Maarten, how are you? I am sorry to bother you but I need your help to sort out a situation with a Sicilian lawyer..."

"I know."

"How do you know? Does everybody around me know everything?"

"Sebastian, is Ms. Lucia with you?"

"Yes, she is in my room."

"Can you please put me through to her?"

"Of course." Puzzled, Sebastian walked toward Lucia. "I know we are dealing with a critical situation, but can you at least talk to a very good friend of mine? He has saved my butt many times and he would like to talk to you."

"Sure, Sebastian. Maybe it will help me figure out something." Laura took the phone from Sebastian's hands. "Hello? This is Lucia Aliberti. How can I help you?" Lucia went back in the hotel room leaving Sebastian on the balcony by himself.

Sebastian wondered if maybe that was the reason he had wanted to be in this business. People can travel in many ways. They all have different expectations and needs. Most of them don't need anybody to take care of them. "Or maybe they do? Maybe what they want is to have someone take care of them for that one time in their lives when they need it."

Lucia joined him again on the balcony. She now looked less insecure than a few minutes earlier. "I have to go."

243

"Why? What did Maarten say?"

"Client-lawyer privilege. I can't share anything more about this case." She kissed him on his forehead.

"What are you talking about, Lucia? I am the one who asked for help first, not Maarten. Aren't you going to help me with the clients anymore?"

"Sebastian. He hired me."

"He... What?"

"He hired me to figure out something for a friend of his."

"Well, I am sure that friend we are talking about is me... Otherwise... Who could he be?"

"She."

"She, who?"

"His friend is a 'she'."

"Who?"

"I can't tell you."

"But what about the boy? What about Laura and John?"

"They will all will be ok. Just stay out of sight for the next 48 hours. And ... Sebastian?"

"Yes."

"Please, nobody listens to me but I do believe in you. Do NOT leave this room until I tell you." Lucia picked up her purse walked toward the door.

"Sounds good. But in three days I'll be back to Minneapolis."

"Three days?" Lucia stopped and turned around looking at Sebastian once more. "I thought you were leaving with John and Laura?"

"No, I want to take a day just for myself."

"All right. We'll talk about that later. I'll call you tomorrow." And with that, Lucia left. Sebastian could hear her heels clicking as she rushed downstairs. He reached for his phone and called Maarten.

"Thank you for calling. I am not available at this time. Please leave a message and I shall call you as soon as possible." If his conversation with Lucia had not been strange enough, not being able to reach out to Maarten was even more peculiar. "I can't believe it. Any time I call him, Maarten answers his phone. Regardless of time zones, hours of the day or meetings."

This was the first time he was going to leave a message. "Maarten, please call me. I don't understand what happened. Is everything ok? Why do you need a lawyer?"

"What am I going to do?" he thought. "Lucia was the only person I knew who could help me figuring out something for the boy..." He went out to the balcony and looked at the sea. Evening was approaching. "It looks so calm. So quiet. Just a few people on the beach; children playing; a guy jogging with his dog ... A blond lady in a white dress walking on the seashore and looking at the horizon, a couple of old sailors smoking cigars..."

"Martina!" Sebastian thought, "Martina Valucelli. Once again!" He went back to his room and opened his backpack. He looked everywhere without finding what he was searching for. "Where is it?"

"Here is my number. Call me if you need help," she had told him. And he had lost it!

He threw on the floor everything he had inside his wallet. No trace of the business card. He did the same with his luggage. "What an idiot!" he thought. Then he remembered that when he had met her, he had a blue jacket. "Maybe.."

He opened the bag with his laundry and found the shirt he was looking for. He checked his breast pocket... "There it is!" He dialed the phone and went to the balcony. He looked for Lucia, but she was already gone. "Darn!"

"Please leave a message after the tone."

"Ms. Valucelli... Ehm ... This is Sebastian. We met a few times in various airports. I just happened to see you here in Sicily...I was wondering if I could talk to you...There is a boy who needs help...Would you please call me back at your earliest convenience?"

Sebastian felt stupid. "That was the most idiotic message I have ever left."

The reply came back very quickly as a text. "Sebastian. This is Martina. I can't talk to you right now, but all has been taken care of. Ms. Lucia Aliberti will call you tomorrow with more details."

Sebastian stared at a silent phone screen. *All is taken care of? How does she know about Lucia?*

Sebastian shouted a Sicilian curse. Seagulls cried as if joining him". He walked back to his room. "She," Laura had said. "Is not a HE but a SHE." Could Maarten know Martina? And how would all of them be connected? Sebastian did the only thing he could come up to. He went to the hotel phone and dialed "0."

"This is Sebastian. I need to talk to Signora Maria."

"This is me, Sebastian. I am on my way."

A knock at the door announced Signora Maria and her son Nico. "I brought you a few things to eat. You sounded worried and I thought you would enjoy some comfort food. Did you have dinner?"

"Actually no," replied Sebastian looking at Nico bringing in plate after plate of delicious food and setting everything on a small table. "I was planning to come downstairs for dinner but a friend of mine stopped by and..."

"I know everything, Sebastian. Eat. Then we can talk. Nico, bring the wine as well, please."

"How bad is it?" Sebastian cut a small slice of provolone cheese and added it to some bread and prosciutto.

"The food?" Signora Maria sat in front of him.

"No. The situation." Sebastian motioned to the display of Sicilian delicatessen set in front of him. "Remember, I was raised by a Sicilian. The bigger the meal, the more complicated the topic." Sebastian, offered her some wine Nico had just brought in but she declined the offer. "She is going to talk for a while," Sebastian thought. As he started to eat, Signora Maria sent Nico back to the first floor of the hotel to take care of the guests.

"Many years ago, I took a trip to Greece with my best friend. We had so many dreams on that summer after Graduation! My best friend's father bought tickets to Greece for both of us. It was our chance to see firsthand the glory of the Classic world. The Greek temples, the ancient cities that once ruled the world, art and history. We would goeverywhere!" She took a small napkin and brought it to the eyes. Where those tears? Sebastian had never seen Signora Maria showing any kind of weakness.

"Everything was perfect. Until we landed in Santorini where we stayed with an old friend of my friend's father. Her hotel was small but beautiful. And the view! Oh, Sebastian, you can't even imagine what it was like waking

246

up every morning and looking at the blue ocean dotted by dozens of white fishing boats."

Sebastian again offered wine, as he thought she might need some. But Signora Maria waved it away energetically. "I am fine. Thank you Sebastian."

"We fell in love, Sebastian. Both of us at the same time. We met two young and beautiful boys from the United States who were on vacation like us and... We fell in love as only young lovers in their first experience can... unconditionally. But life can be so cruel. It can quickly transform moments of blissed happiness into desperation."

"What happened, Signora Maria? If you were so happy, what could possibly happen to impact your life so dramatically?"

"I got pregnant."

Sebastian choked on a golf-ball size arancino. Signora Maria promptly got behind him and did the Heimlich move. "Seriously Sebastian, this is not the time to choke to death. Wait until I'm done!" Once Sebastian recovered, she sat back down on her chair. Sebastian drank a large glass of water.

"I got pregnant. But I didn't tell my friend. I stayed behind on the island pretending I was having too much fun to leave. My friend left, but asked me to promise her to not stay too long, as college would start in a few weeks."

"What about the father?"

Signora Maria stopped and drank some water. "I thought about telling him. But he was so young. He had so many dreams... Like I did. We spent many a night looking at the stars, asking them to witness our absolute love and commitment to each other. On his last day on the island, we promised each other to write and stay connected. He would come and visit Sicily the following summer... I never told him I was pregnant... And he never wrote to me." Signora Maria stopped to dry a tear with a napkin.

"How did you and the child survive?"

"The British lady who was hosting me took care of us. She taught me everything she knew about how to tend to customers and hotel management. Eventually, I got married. And with my then husband, we opened our first hotel... And life went on. We survived."

Signora Maria finally stood up. "The point is, Sebastian, that when you least expect, help will come. I know you want to help your clients. But this is the time for you to let it go for a while. There are many people who are trying to help right now. You would just be on their way."

"What should I do?"

"Stay here for the next 48 hours. I'll have Nico bring you food and everything you need. Other than that, just be ready. At some point you will be needed again. I am sure about that."

"Thank you Signora Maria."

"You are a good man, Sebastian. You and your friends are going to change three lives... As some people changed my life many years ago. Buona notte Sebastian. Good night."

"Signora Maria?"

"Yes, Sebastian?"

"Your first child. What did you tell him about his father?"

"That he had died when he was an infant."

"Have you ever told him the truth?"

"Too late, Sebastian. Too late. But that is a story for another time. Good night Bastianeddu.

# CHAPTER LXI

## *Pensione Mirabella, Acireale, Sicily*

The morning light found Laura and John holding each other in bed. They had spent the night talking about their future and the endless possible outcomes for their adventure. On one thing they both agreed: the boy would remain part of their lives. They did not know how yet, but they felt his life was now connected to theirs.

Signora Maria had moved them to the largest room she had available: a suite with two beds, a dining table, a sofa and a small kitchen. To the boy, used to spending his time in the hull of a boat or the closet of a church, all this space made him feel like he was living in a castle. But even though he could sleep on his own bed, he chose to spend the night on top of the rug they had brought from church. "It smells right," he said.

"Look at him," Laura said, looking down from her comfortable bed. "Our little Angel is still sleeping. All bundled in covers and pillows."

"I can't even imagine what he must have gone through." John looked at Laura. "He is our second chance. We are not going to leave him behind."

"I am scared, John."

"Why?"

"I don't want him to get the illusion of a new family only to later fail again. What if we can't take him with us?"

"Think about the opposite."

"What?"

"What are we planning to do with him once we get back home? A world

249

of opportunities will be open to him."

"Incoming call from Lucia Aliberti" announced John's Concierge. "It's her," said John! "She must have a plan!"

"Hi John, this is Lucia. How did you three sleep?"

"Let's say the night was not long enough. Angels are still sleeping."

"Great! How long do you think it will take you to get ready? Is one hour enough?"

"Depends. Ready for what?"

"A drive to Palermo, a meeting at the U.S. Consulate and a flight back to the U.S."

"Wait. There must be a mistake. Our flight is not until tomorrow. We have a full day..."

"No, you have been re-booked for tonight. Your flight leaves from Palermo at 5:00 p.m. And we have lots to do before then. I'll be there in 58 minutes."

"I thought you said one hour?"

"57 minutes." Laura hung up her call and dialed a new number.

\* \* \*

"Come on, Sebastian. Wake up!"

"Hello? This is Sebastian..."

"It's me. Lucia. I'll be at the Hotel in thirty minutes. I need you to sign a few papers and make a copy of your Italian passport."

"Wait. What are you talking about? Why would you need my Italian passport?"

"Don't worry. Just have that ready and pack up your luggage. We are going to Palermo. Your flight leaves tomorrow morning at 7:00 a.m. from Palermo.

"Palermo? Tomorrow? My flight is in two days. And I leave from Catania."

"That was before we made the change. I'll be there in a few minutes."

"But wait! I need to close my bill... Say goodbye to Signora Maria..."

"All taken care of. Please Sebastian. Get your stuff organized."

Sebastian called the front desk. "Hi, this is Sebastian. May I speak with

Signora Maria?"

"I am sorry," replied somebody at the front desk he could not recognize. "Signora Maria had to take care of some business."

"What about Nico?"

"He is driving Signora Maria. They told me to tell you that they look forward to seeing you again soon. Your room has been taken care of and your ride to Palermo has been arranged for. The driver will pick you up in about half an hour. Do you need any help with your luggage?"

"No, thank you."

Sebastian hang off the phone and started packing. He didn't have much but his few belongings were spread all over the place. "I should call Gerard to let him know about the new booking but it's too late in the night in the United States. A text should do the work for now."

\* \* \*

"All right, we're all set, Laura. I don't think I've forgotten anything. We still have a few minutes to spare. What about some breakfast?"

"I think that's a great idea" said Laura coming out of the bathroom in a full Grace Kelly-like long, white summer dress. "What do you think about this outfit for our meeting with the U.S. Consul?"

"I am sure he, or she, is going to be speechless!"

"It's just the flush of happiness. You also look very handsome. I don't really know what I'll to do without these clothes. I'll have to find out where they ordered them."

"And the best thing is we don't have to take them with us. I kept a few items for the trip to the U.S. But other than that, the only thing I had to do was to put them in a laundry bag. They will be shipped back to the tailor... And now... look at this little one!" John pointed to the little boy. "The clothes that Signora Maria brought us for him are just perfect. He looks like a little model!"

"He does! Now, the three of us, let's take a final look at the Mediterranean." She bent down and hugged the little boy. "Your parents must be very proud of you. You have endured so much. I promise you we are always going to be together. Would you like that?"

The boy smiled and nodded. "Yes," he said. Then he blew a kiss to the sea. "Bye mum, bye dad, bye-bye brother and sister. I love you."

# CHAPTER LXII

## *Pensione Mirabella, Acireale, Sicily*

A loud knock at the door announced Lucia Aliberti. "Sebastian, it's me, please open the door. We don't have much time!"

Sebastian opened the door. Backpack and luggage ready. "Here is the mystery girl! Can you please explain…"

"Please stop talking. The less you know, the better. Let me take a picture of the passport with my phone … Perfect. And, sent. Thank you technology!"

"Where are you sending the data?"

"Jesus! She told me you would be a pain. I just did not know you would act this way under stress."

"What stress? And who talked to you? I am not stressed! I just would like to know what is going on!"

"Here. Read this message. But firts, sign this document." Lucia showed Sebastian a tablet with a document requiring electronic signature.

"What is it?"

"Do you trust me?"

"Of course I do. But…"

"No 'But.' Just sign. Please Sebastian, I have no time."

"Ok, ok. But if you screw up my finances more than they are right now, you will have to deal with my financial advisor in person. And she is NOT going to forgive you. I promise," He said while signing the electronic document.

"Don't worry. No financial implications. All will be fine. Now you can read the message I gave you."

Sebastian opened the message. It was from Martina Valucelli.

"Dear Sebastian, I have hired Ms. Aliberti to help us. Please do trust her. We are all trying to do our best to give the child a future."

"Lucia, this still does not make any sense. But I trust you and Ms. Valucelli to do the right thing. What next?"

"For you? Nothing. Your ride to Palermo is waiting downstairs. He'll drive you to your hotel. Please, just remain in your room until tomorrow morning when the same driver will pick you up to take you to the airport."

Lucia gave him an envelope. "Here is your new ticket to Minneapolis. First class."

"I guess Ms. Valucelli has taken care of everything... How ironic that somebody would setup logistic arrangements for an expert in travel."

"Yes, it is funny," smiled Lucia. "Sebastian, I really wish we had more time..."

"I know. Next time I'll stay longer. I promise."

Lucia hugged Sebastian. "I am so glad I bumped into you a few days ago... One last thing. Please do NOT call anybody until you get back to your home in the United States... Promise me."

"I promise you, Lucia."

"Ciao, ciao Sebastian." Lucia walked to the elevator and stopped for a moment. Then changed her mind and took the steps to the ground floor.

"Bye Lucia." Sebastian went back to his room and picked up his luggage. Once downstairs, he found a limo waiting for him. A second one was parked just behind.

He opened the door of his vehicle and sat back. Signora Maria had said, "There are many people who are trying to help right now. This is the time for you to let go for a while. You would just be on their way."

He smiled. "She already knew everything." He smiled.

# PART XIII

*How love mends two lost souls with angel*

# CHAPTER LXIII

*Pensione Mirabella, Acireale, Sicily*

"All right little man! Are you ready?" Lucia bent down and looked in his eyes. "So much hope and happiness!" she thought, trying to master her emotions. Then, to Laura and John "Did you gather all your belongings?"

"Yes," answered John. "We are ready to go."

"Perfect. Let's get into the car. It will take about two hours to get to Palermo. I'll explain you everything on our way to the U.S. Embassy."

John and Laura thanked the personnel of Pensione Mirabella. "I was hoping to say goodbye to Signora Maria and Nico…"

"I am really sorry," replied the Manager on duty. "They had some business to take care of. But they want you to know that they look forward to seeing you back soon."

"This place has been very important to our…family" said Laura. "You can bet we'll be back again."

The four of them got into a large, black limousine. "Ms. Valucelli though you would be more comfortable during the trip," said Lucia. "Why don't you relax a bit, first? We can have some water, soda…Maybe some relaxing music? We have plenty of time for details."

"Sure, Lucia. I am also sure this little one has never been on such a big car. Have you?" Laura asked the little boy who was meanwhile testing all different seats available inside the vehicle.

The car drove south, passing by Catania "The industrial core of Sicily.

Founded by both Sicilians and Greeks. Beautiful churches and palaces built by Spanish, ancient theaters hidden under lava and the buildings of the new city. And the beach! You have to come back and stop by, next time" said Lucia. With a turn westward, the driver entered the freeway to Palermo, the old Capital city of the old Kingdom of the two Sicilies.

"I really don't know how I am going to do this," Lucia thought. "They are going to hate me ...but I have to do it before we get to the Embassy..." Laura picked up a bottle of water from one of the refrigerators available in the limo. She looked at the little boy. His face attached to the window: eyes wide open, looking out to the sea. "John, Laura, we need to talk."

"Sure!" said John holding Laura's hand and smiling. "What kind of information is the Consulate going to ask us to get the adoption process started to allow us to bring Angelo back to the United States?"

"Before I start, I want to make sure I have your full trust in me." Lucia looked at both Laura and John in the eyes.

"Of course, Lucia. You've been so close to us. And now that Ms. Valucelli has hired you as the baby's lawyer, I am sure everything will be ok." Laura said, moving closer to the boy.

"Perfect. We are all working together in the interest of the boy." Laura drank some water. "And in the interest of the boy and everybody involved, I won't be able to share all information I have as we go through the process."

John and Lucia looked at each other, then nodded.

"I need you to remember that I represent the boy. And the boy only. Not the three of you." Continued Lucia. "Now, going back to our meeting at the Consulate. We are going to meet with the Consul but not to talk about adoptions. We, the boy and I, are going to get a passport."

"Of course, Lucia. We need his passport so we can get him into the United States," John smiled relieved.

"Here is the point." Lucia took a deep breath. "You two are not going to be the ones getting the boy through immigration."

"What? What are you saying, Lucia? We are not going to leave the boy in Italy! This is madness... John?" Laura looked at him with hopeful eyes.

"Let her finish, Laura."

Lucia took another glass of water. She looked at the boy, who was now feeling the anger and tension inside the car. She clicked on the speakerphone connecting her to the driver. "Please take the exit for the Sicily Outlet Village and stop by the side entrance."

"As you wish, Madam. The next exit is in just two miles."

"That will be perfect. Thank you," Lucia picked up her phone and typed a message.

"John, Laura, I need to talk to him for a few minutes. Alone. We are going to stop and I'll talk to him outside." Then she turned to Angelo.

"Are you ok with that? Everything will be fine. I just need to talk to you in private."

The boy nodded and looked at John and Laura. "It's going to be ok," John said stroking the boy's hair. "We'll be waiting for you here."

Silence fell on the travelers. The excitement had morphed into anxiety. The limousine took the exit leading to the most luxurious shopping mall on the island and stopped by the side entrance. Lucia took the boy's hand and helped him out of the car.

Laura and John saw them walking up a large marble staircase with a glamorous jewelry store on the top. Lucia sat on a bench with Angelo, gave him some water and started talking. After a few minutes, they entered the jewelry store.

"I don't know Laura. But I trust Lucia and Ms. Valucelli. They wouldn't do anything to hurt us. I'm sure of that." He walked toward the bar area of the limo and filled two glasses with chinotto, his newly discovered Sicilian drink. He gave a glass to Laura and looked outside. "Look, another limousine on its way to this mall …"

Laura went to the window. "For some reason I feel that this isn't a coincidence."

The second limousine approached Laura and John's and parked alongside. The back window came down just a little bit. "Sir, Madam," said Laura and John's driver", the guest from the other limo would like to talk to you."

"Of course", said John. He pushed the switch and took down his window. Martina Valucelli smiled to both of them.

258

"Thank you John and Laura. I am really sorry for the way we are meeting, but this is the safest path for everybody. This way nobody will be able to see any connection between us."

"Martina," Laura started. "Thank you so much for your help. But I am really confused."

"It is confusing, but trust me. This is the only way to give the little boy a new home. Now, listen. We don't have much time. We must be in Palermo right on time for both our appointments."

"Appointments?" asked John.

"Lucia will tell you everything that will happen during your meeting with the Consul. For what concerns mine, I can't tell you anything. You will have to trust me."

"Of course, Martina. What do you want us to do?"

"I need you to do something that will break your heart. But if you believe in me and Lucia, everything will be fine at the end."

"I don't understand," said John. "What can we give you?"

"The little boy. You need to let the boy come with me."

"To the Embassy?" Laura began to sob.

"To the United States. It's the only option. If we don't do it this way, the boy will be sent back to his home. And we won't be able to do anything for him."

"No!" Screamed Laura. "John! We can't let her take our child away! Not again!"

John looked at Laura. "It's not about us, Laura. It's about him. If we love him, we need to let him go with Martina and trust her."

"Laura, I know you hate me right now. But please, believe me. I am doing this for all of you." Martina picked up her phone and typed a message. "Lucia has already talked to the boy. He is going to get into my limousine. Lucia will join you instead. When we meet again in Palermo, you will have to act like you have never met me before. Promise."

Laura cried, "I must say goodbye! I must see him again!" John held her back.

"Yes, Martina. We'll follow Lucia's directions. Our future is in your hands."

"Thank you, John." Martina closed her window and told the driver to back up a bit. Just enough to allow Lucia to open the door and help the boy into the limousine. Lucia hugged him and closed the door. To the eyes of the personnel of the jewelry store and the other people visiting the shopping center, a very wealthy child, accompanied by his nanny, had purchased something extremely valuable and then left in his limo while his nanny had gone home with her own luxurious vehicle.

"That's how royalty lives," thought the store manager.

# CHAPTER LXI

### *Sicilia Outlet Village, Agira, Sicily*

Lucia got back in the limousine to find John trying to console a distraught Laura. She closed the door and directed the driver to speed toward the U.S. Consulate in Palermo.

"I trusted you!" screamed Laura. "I thought you were on our side! You betrayed us! You betrayed the boy too! What's going to happen to him?"

"Laura, I am really sorry. But this was the only way to save him. It only started because you called the U.S. Embassy in Rome letting them know you found the boy when I warned both of you not to do so..."

"Why would calling the Embassy be such a horrible thing? We are U.S. citizens!" cried Laura.

"You are, but the boy is not. The call to the Embassy in Rome put an immediate spotlight on you two. Every security agent by now expects you to show up at the border with a boy. Do you know what would happen?"

"Worst case scenario they would send him back to his home?"

"Yes. But his home is not Italy. I don't even know where his home is. And wherever his home is, It would not be a good thing for a boy his age to be sent back without adults to protect him."

"So. What's going to happen now?" John asked.

"Where did you see the boy first, John?"

"The fish market."

"Perfect. You are going to the Consulate to officially declare that you have found the boy at the fish market and that you immediately recognized he

261

did not belong there." Lucia picked up a clean handkerchief from her purse. "Laura, the Consul will ask you how you found his family. You will tell her what you shared with me. But just the basics. The boy talked about an accident with a boat which led him to fall into the sea and find his way to where you found him. You have no other details to share with the exception of Ms. Valucelli's business card. The phone company has a record of your call to her cell and the voicemail you left refers to your finding her business card."

Lucia went suddenly quiet and silence fell inside the limousine.

John took a deep breath and started "If I follow what you are saying, we called Ms. Valucelli to let her know that we had found a boy who had some kind of relationship with her. As if she was his..."

"His mother," whispered Lucia.

"No!" cried Laura. "She can't take him away from me. She has everything! Why would she want him too?"

"As his mother, she has already petitioned for an U.S. passport. She was very young when she had the boy and, to protect her social status, she could not share any news of him. For this reason, she left Angelo with his father. A father who has both Italian and U.S. passports. Now that she has found the boy again, she is going to take him back home. But she needs a U.S. passport to do so. And very quickly."

"The boy has a father?" asked John.

"Yes, but he has given up his rights to the child effective when he reaches his destination in the United States."

"Where?" asked Laura.

"I can't disclose this information as it is specifically related to the boy. And he is my client."

"How can Martina get a new passport if the boy was never registered in the U.S. as her child?"

"This is something you will have to ask Martina," said Lucia. "Are we all on the same page? Can you ensure me you will just tell the truth? Well... an edited version of the truth? Remember. We are doing all this to give a future to Angelo"

John looked at Laura. Their eyes met and connected as only two people who are in love and know everything of each other can. "Yes, Lucia."

The three of them remained silent for the remainder of the journey to Palermo.

...

"Incoming call from Maarten," announced Sebastian's device, waking him up suddenly. "Maarten, how are you? Where are you calling from this time?"

"Listen, I just wanted to thank you for personally introducing me to Ms. Lucia. She is amazing."

"I know. I wish I had the chance to thank her. The last 24 hours have been quite hectic. I still can't believe this trip is over. One last night in Palermo and I'll be on my way back to boredom."

"Well, it does not have to be that way, Sebastian. If your customers are happy with you, they will refer more business to you."

"Maarten, it will take me years to recover financially from this trip..."

"Nonsense. I am sure all expenses will be taken care of...and more. I need to ask you another favor. Can you meet Lucia at the airport, tomorrow? It is a precaution. Just in case."

"Just in case what?"

"I can't tell you right now. But, please be at the airport on time for your flight."

"Sure Maarten, thank you."

"No, Sebastian... Thank YOU. I have finally realized something was missing in my life..."

"Maarten, are you ok?"

"Nothing, Sebastian. I'll talk to you when you land in the U.S. Bye Sebastian. Have a great trip back home. And remember, life is never as bad as it seems."

"And we only get one to live... Thank you Maarten. And you have a great trip as well...Wherever you are..."

# CHAPTER LXII

*Palermo, Sicily*

T he limousine finally got into Palermo. When it passed the Norman cathedral of Monreale, Lucia prayed that the Cristo Pantocreatore would that he could bless them all with his right-hand's golden mosaic three fingers[20] made of golden mosaics. They drove through the richest areas of the city, Old mansions lining both sides of the street. When they got to the Consulate, the limousine did not stop.

"Are we looking for a parking spot, Lucia?" John asked.

"No, we are actually going to stop a bit further away." She motioned him to wait and avoid other questions.

The driver turned a few times until he entered an underground parking lot. He went down a few levels, then stopped near a car.

"Lucia! Is that our…"

"Yes, Laura. That is your rental car. The one you had left at Pensione Mirabella."

"How did it get here, Lucia?"

"Somebody must have known that you needed a car that was not as flashy as a limousine for your meeting with the Consul." Lucia smiled.

"Signora Maria," said John. "Of course. She must have driven our car to Palermo and Nico must have driven his own car so they could get back home after their mission."

"That may be possible, John. Of course, I would not know," said Lucia. But I would be surprised if the keys were inside the car. That would be too risky. Sometimes, when I have to, I leave the keys under one of my front wheels."

John opened the door and got out of the limousine. He walked to the rental car, and bent down. Hidden under the left front wheel was the car key. He smiled and showed the keys to Laura and Lucia. "Bingo.!"

Lucia turned to Laura. "I know you are very concerned right now. But I need you to trust me and Ms. Valucelli. Please follow the plan and just tell the story as rehearsed inside the limo. Also remember that you have been so distraught by everything that has happened that you have decided to go back to the United State one day earlier than planned."

"Of course. Thank you Lucia for everything you have done." Laura picked up her backpack, then looked at Lucia one last time, "Shall I see you again?"

---

[20] Reference to the Trinity

"Maybe. One day. Who knows? Enjoy your trip back home, Laura. Your new tickets are inside the car. You can leave the car at the Departures valet line. The personnel at the airport has been already notified."

"Thank you, Lucia." Laura got out of the limousine and joined John inside the rental car.

\* \* \*

Everything that happened next seemed to Laura like it was happening to someone she was observing from the safe, comfortable chair of a movie theater.

John had found a perfect parking spot near the Consulate. The State Department personnel received them like they were some kind of heroes. "You have saved the boy from a very uncertain and dangerous situation. He could have been lost for months. You should be very proud of what you have done!" said the Consul, thanking them on behalf of Ms. Valucelli and the U.S. Government.

The Italian police escorted them all the way to the airport to make sure they arrived in time for their flight to Amsterdam and then the United States. The security team at the airport had set up a special screening and transfer to the plane. Once in Amsterdam, they were escorted to their connection to the United States. Even the security screening in Minneapolis was uneventful. When the immigration officer scanned their passports he just said, "Welcome home."

"Everybody knew. Lucia was right." Sitting in her living room, a glass of Sicilian white wine in her hand, Laura had realized that the right or wrong move with the Consulate would have decided the fate of the boy.

Laura walked outside and breathed in the smell of purple Russian sage she had planted all around the house. John was cutting the grass, although he really didn't have to do as a team of professionals took care of the yard. But it was John's way to easing his anxiety. She gave him a glass of wine. "Let's drink to whatever the future will bring to us, John."

"Cheers! Bring it on!" said John.

"Incoming message from Sebastian," announced Maria, John's device.

"Are you still wearing your device, John?"

"Oh yes, I just had it in my back pocket as a reminder that I need to return both phones to the Travel Company. Let me check the message. It's probably our bill."

John read the message and then looked at Laura.

"What does it say?" Asked Laura.

"I am outside your door."

"The front door? Who? Sebastian? The owner of the company?

"No. Angelo."

# CHAPTER LXIII

*Palermo, Sicily*

For once, Sebastian had followed instructions. In Palermo, he checked into the hotel chosen by Lucia and had stayed there- He even had dinner brought to his room to avoid any contact with other people. His taxi, scheduled in advance by Lucia, took him quickly to the airport where he found out that an express check-in and security screening had been set up for him.

He picked up his phone and texted his flight information to Gerard, Fernando and Gloria.

*Can't wait to see Gerard again. I really need to talk to him. Maybe this is the right time for us.*

He checked the time. "Still a long way to go," he thought. "Maybe I should take a walk around." He was packing his backpack when he heard a commotion in the distance.

"Lightning. Inside the airport?" Sebastian thought. "Maybe some kind of electrical malfunction?"

He saw a couple of shadows entering a side door and a few seconds later a large group of people came out of a corner. They were all running and shouting

"Damn! I lost her!" said one of them. "I swear! She has a boy with her." He shouted to a cameraman.

"There's no way. She couldn't have pulled off a pregnancy and a birth without anybody knowing it," said a man with a mike on his hand.

"Look, somebody's at that gate. Let's ask him!"

Sebastian realized too late that he was now the target of the group. The camera man switched on lights and cameras while his colleague activated his large microphone.

"Sir. Have you seen her? Have you seen a boy? How did she look? Why were they running?"

"I have no idea what you are talking about." started Sebastian. "Who are you looking for?"

"Ms. Valucelli," answered the reporter. "We saw her running this way with another person. They had a young boy with them. Have you seen them? Were they all together? Who is the mother? Are they lesbians?"

"Stop right now," Sebastian replied. "I was on the phone a few minutes ago when I saw a few shadows running that direction," he said, pointing to the far end of the terminal opposite where the group was coming from.

Frustrated, the reporters, paparazzi (or both) switched off cameras and microphones and started running again. Sebastian remained seated for a few minutes, then he started walking toward the location where he thought he had seen three people disappear.

"Incoming call from Lucia Aliberti," announced his device. "For some reason, I think I know what is going on," thought Sebastian. He picked up the phone and before he could answer Lucia started.

"Sebastian! I need your help! Plan B is needed. Please come over right now."

"Where are you, Lucia?"

"We are in the family bathroom near Gate 25 ..."

"I see the sign and I think I know where you are. I'm on my way."

"Make sure nobody is following you. Knock at the door and we shall come out."

"Sure." He walked toward the family bathroom door and looked around. With the exception of a couple of cleaning crew members, nobody was around. He knocked at the door. Lucia and the little boy came out, closing the door behind them.

"Lucia, Is everything ok? What is going on?"

"Plan A did not work. Somebody must have called the press. They were waiting for us just behind the security checkpoint. We barely made it here before it was too late. We need to activate Plan B."

"Which is?"

"You won't like it."

"Why?"

"It involves you."

"I don't understand"

"Martina's team is already changing your flight schedule. You are going to take her place on the next flight to Rome later today. She is going to take your seat on the flight to Amsterdam instead so she can leave the airport as soon as possible. Nobody can see her with the little boy."

"Of course … But … Aren't you the boy's lawyer? You can take him to the United States."

"No, I need to help Martina leave the airport."

"Who is going to take the boy to the United States?"

"You are."

"Me?"

"Yes."

"Are you crazy? Immigration will never let me enter the country with a boy not related to me. They will think I have kidnapped him or something worse!"

"Sebastian, calm down. Nobody will question you. You are…his father."

"What!?"

The paparazzi and cameramen appeared again, in the distance.

"Angelo, please take Sebastian's hand and mine. We are going to look like a normal family travelling somewhere. Please, both of you smile!"

The three of them walked toward the gate. A cloud of angry and sweaty people approached and passed through them.

"Damn! I swear I thought I saw her. She must be hidden somewhere! Can you ladies check in the bathrooms?"

"Are you out of your mind, you moron? There's a limit to the invasion of a person's privacy! With that said, I actually need to go to the ladies."

"I knew it! You are going to use the fact that you can check the ladies' bathroom to find her and get the exclusive!"

"Well, if you want to go into the ladies' bathrooms, be my guest. There are security cameras, though, I must warn you. You could lose your license..." Smiling, she went into the women's bathroom and walked away.

"That woman! I hate her! She gets her way all the time!"

The group walked away. John, Lucia and the little boy remained seated until the woman came out of the ladies' bathroom.

"Sebastian, you must go to Gate 15. They will have your new tickets by now. I need to go back to Martina."

"Wait! How can I be his father?"

"This is what his passport states. He is your and Martina's child. Laura and John found him after an accident at sea. He was in Sicily all of his life but now Martina is taking him back to the U.S."

"And what am I supposed to do with him once we get to the U.S.?"

Laura gave Sebastian a large envelope. "You have to take him to the address specified in this document. Please open it only after you pass immigration. Not knowing what will happen to the boy after the Immigration point is better for you." Then she looked at Angelo. "You are such an incredible boy. I'll miss you so much. Please follow Sebastian. He is a good guy and will take care of you. Stay with him all the time, ok?"

The boy nodded and smiled. "Mi mancherai. I'll miss you!" He gave her a hug and took Sebastian's hand.

"Lucia, I'll miss you too. I'll take care of him."

"You better do. Otherwise my mother will never forgive me."

"Your mother? Who is your mother, Lucia?"

"You are the dumbest Sicilian I have ever met. Signora Maria. She is my mother. Haven't you realized we have the same last name?"

"No. I have always called her Signora Maria. I actually thought her last name was Mirabella. Like in Pensione Mirabella."

"Oh my goodness, Sebastiano. Mirabella is the Sicilian city where she was born!"

"Oh. So Signora Maria's last name is Aliberti?"

"Sebastian! Aliberti is my husband's last name. I have known you since you were born and you don't even remember my last name?"

"You know me since I was born?"

"Yes, Sebastian. I was even your babysitter on the day your mother passed. Don't you remember? You, Nico and I were playing on the beach."

Sebastian focused on few fragments of his past.

Lucia pinched both Sebastian's cheeks "Beddu ma babbu.[21]"

Angelo giggled.

"Sebastian, my maiden name is Lucia della Lunga. Nico and I are the youngest children. Your father is our oldest brother."

Sebastian looked lost in thoughts. "That means..."

"That means that I am your aunt and Signora Maria is your grandmother." Lucia looked at Angelo. "And technically Angelo is part of our family as well... At least until you land in the United States."

"I don't understand," started Sebastian.

Lucia looked around and typed something on her phone. "Sebastian. For now please focus on Angelo. Once everything is set in place, please call your father. You two need to have a long talk. I have to go Sebastiano." She gave him a big hug.

In the far distance, a female figure came out of a door and walked toward the business lounge. Lucia ran toward her. A tear marked her face.

---

[21] Handosme but stupid

# CHAPTER LXIV

*On the Way Home*

"Are you ok?" Sebastian asked little Angelo.

"Si, yes," answered the boy and turned back to the window, hand holding tight the chain Signora Carmela had given him. Outside, fluffy clouds dotted the sky like flying cotton sheep.

"Only two hours to our landing in Minneapolis," Sebastian thought while filling out his immigration paperwork. According to his passport, Angelo had three last names: Sebastian's, Valucelli and...Robinson. "This is weird. I wonder if Valucelli is just her alias name and Robinson is her real last name."

"Ladies and Gentlemen, we are now approaching Minneapolis-St. Paul..."

"Robinson... Why does this last name sound familiar..." Sebastian checked his and Angelo's tables and chairs. He collected all of their belongings and put them in his backpack. "Angelo, we are almost home. Are you happy?"

The boy smiled.

Sebastian sat back and closed his eyes. "I really need to send a huge thank you note to everybody who has helped me for this trip. Especially Maarten... He sounded weird during our last call. What did he say? Life is never as bad as it seems..." When had he heard a similar saying? Was that before leaving for Italy?

"Martina!" He opened his eyes. "Martina told me something similar..." Martina Valucelli... Martina Valucelli Robinson ... Robinson ... Rob'nSon... . Could Martina and Rob be related?"

He tried to remember his visit to Rob's store. "Beautiful clothes everywhere... Italian paintings... Marble floors ... A captivating scent of lavender... The smell! Like Martina's perfume!"

"My sister owns a factory in France. That is where we get all of our perfumes..." Robert had told him.

Sebastian picked up his phone but the hostess scolded him. "Usage of electronics is absolutely forbidden right now!"

"Ok, this theory is insane. But Maarten and Martina will hear from me as soon as I get home," he thought.

The plane landed. Sebastian and Angelo walked to the immigration checkpoint. "Auch! I forgot to send another message with my new flight information to everybody," thought Sebastian. "I better do that as soon as I am out of the secure zone.

Sebastian and Angelo walked toward the section dedicated to "U.S. citizens". He was nervous but he had rehearsed his part many time.

"Good afternoon, sir," he started.

"Passports, please."

"Sure. Here they are."

"Who do we have here? Mr. Sebastian della Lunga and... Little boy, and you are?"

"Angelo"

"He is my son." Sebastian smiled nervously.

"Uhm. Let me check your passport...Here it is...Angelo...Wow. Three last names? Robinson, Valucelli, and ... Wait! Valucelli. Are you related to ..."

The boy nodded smiling.

"And you are the father?"

"Yes. Any issue with his passport?"

"No, no. Sir you two need to be escorted immediately."

"Why?" Sebastian started sweating profusely.

"Beyond my pay grade." The immigration officer called his office and exchanged a few sentences Sebastian and Angelo could not hear. He then approached Sebastian. "A car is waiting for both of you outside the airport...

274

Sir, little boy, I am really sorry. I really am," He called the security team. "They are on their way."

The boy started getting nervous and squeezed Sebastian's hand. "Everything is going to be all right, Angelo. There must be a misunderstanding."

The security agents escorted Sebastian and Angelo through a secondary door. It wasn't much distant from the main exit. But far enough to allow unnoticed passage.

A policewoman was carrying a small dog with her. "Emotional Support" written on a bandana it carried on his neck. "Do you like dogs?" she asked the boy.

He nodded back.

"Would you like to hold him? You can, if you want." Angelo smiled and picked up the dog who immediately snuggled with him. "Perfect. Hold him like this. He gets scared when too many people are around him."

As soon as they exited the secure zone, Sebastian and Angelo were hit by loud cries and agitated conversations. Large TV crews were set up near the main exit from the secure zone. A KARE11 correspondent was talking to a camera. "We don't know all the details yet. The accident is still under investigation and the authorities are not confirming anything at the moment. The only thing we know, is that the front of the airplane is the part that got most of the damage. First and business class passengers are among the casualties."

The boy looked at Sebastian, looking for answers. "Looks like there was some kind of airplane accident," he told Angelo. "Let me check if I can find more information". Sebastian asked one of the security guards who were escorting them for more details, but the guard did not reply beyond a somber and sad look to the boy.

The guards created a wall on both sides of Sebastian and Angelo, like a protective screen from the external world. A black limousine was waiting for them outside the airport. The officer in charge walked toward the driver. The policewoman got closer to the boy.

"You can keep the dog with you for a couple of days. Would you like that? I can pick him up at any time."

Angelo smiled and looked at Sebastian. Without exchanging a word, Sebastian looked at the policewoman who closed her eyes and signaled him to go inside the car. "All of this can't be good," he thought. "Yes, you can keep him. I'll call his owner and arrange for its pick up in a few days. Now, let's get into the car."

They entered the limousine and thanked the security team. For what, they still did not know.

"Good morning, sir," said the driver via speaker phone. Please enjoy the ride. We'll get to our destination in about 45 minutes."

"Can you tell us where we are going?" said Sebastian.

"I'm sorry. I've been told not to do so."

"Sounds good. Thank you." Sebastian realized his phone was still switched off. He looked at the boy and noticed that he was happily playing with the dog. "Good time to reactivate my phone."

Once switched on, the phone started beeping without coming to an end. Message after message. Voicemail after voicemail. Even his social media and whatsup accounts seemed to go into overload. Everybody was asking if he was fine or where he was. Before he could even dial a number, the first call came in.

"Incoming call from Gloria McDonald, Sebastian."

"Gloria, How?"

"Oh my God! Sebastian! Are you ok?"

"Yes, I am. Why? What happened?"

"Are you still in shock? Your flight had a mechanical accident while landing in O'Hare. The entire front of the plane smashed to the ground! My God! Where are you? Which hospital? I am on my way to the airport."

"Wait! I'm fine. I ended up taking a different flight. I just landed in Minneapolis and I'm actually on my way home."

"I thought I was going to die! Why didn't you send me the new itinerary?"

"I didn't think it was that important. I thought nobody would be interested."

"I'm your friend, idiot! Of course I am interested. Gerard, Fernando and your family are a mess. You better call them right now!"

"Sure. Thank you Gloria. I'll call you later."

Sebastian made a few quick calls to let everybody know that he was safe. He finally called Gerard. "Hi Gerard, it's me."

"Honest to God. If you don't die on your own before you get back home, for sure I'll take care of that. I just talked to Gloria. Why didn't you call me or send a message?"

"Well, I thought you were still upset about using your phone without telling you..."

"Of course I'm mad about that! You better get home soon."

"I will. But first I need to do something. I promise I won't be late."

"Sure! Until a few hours ago I thought I would have to take care of your funeral. Now I just have to find out the legal way to kill you. Get your ass home!"

"There you have it. My lovely Gerard is back. Ciao!" Sebastian hang off and opened the envelope that Lucia had given him. It contained two smaller envelops marked with numbers. "Leave it to Lucia to put in order even the way I need to open the envelopes!"

He opened the envelope marked with the number "1". It was from Martina Valucelli.

*Dear Sebastian,*

*If you have opened this envelope, it means that our plan A has failed.*

*First, let me thank you for the incredible opportunity you have given me. For my entire life, I had to carefully plan every single minute as every action I took was under scrutiny. You and Lucia have allowed me to be part of something bigger. Something that went beyond preserving my own life and privacy. Something that required me to take an incredible risk.*

*By now, you will probably be on your way to the boy's final destination. You can't even imagine how both challenging and exhilarating it has been to be able to get him to this point. I'll reconnect with you in a few days. For now, the only thing you need to know is that I have declared that you are his father –and you may have already realized it when you passed your Immigration interview.*

*As his mother, I was able to get him a U.S. passport. However, our role as parents of Angelo will end as soon as you will get to the destination. The second envelope contains the release of our parental rights. I trust you will give the second envelope to the people you meet at the destination.*

*There is so much that I would like you to know, but I don't have much time.*

*I shall connect with you soon,*
  *Martina Valucelli*

"Release of parental rights? That's it! That is what Lucia made me sign," thought Sebastian.

"Sir, we are in the subdivision. We'll be at the destination in a few minutes" announced the driver. Sebastian looked outside the window and smiled. He recognized his neighborhood. He definitely knew where he was going. He looked at the boy. All tucked into the back of the limo with his new dog. Both asleep.

"Angelo," he whispered on his ear. "Angelo, we are home."

The boy opened his eyes. He looked at Sebastian and at his little snoring new treasure. He stood up and looked out the window. Children playing in a large park. Couples walking on the sidewalks. It all looked like a dream. They finally arrived at the end of a cul-de-sac.

"Sir, I won't be able to get into the private driveway with this car. I am really sorry. It is too long."

"I know, I'll walk him there. I am sure the little dog will appreciate a small walk as well. How much do I owe you?"

"Well, first of all, the trip has been already paid. Second, we still have to go to another place before I can drive you home."

"Where are we... Oh! I guess you won't be able to tell me?"

"No, I am really sorry, sir. I'll wait here for you to come back."

"Sure. I'll see you in a few minutes."

Sebastian and Angelo walked down a street with only three homes. It was just a man, a small boy and a little dog. But they felt like an army coming home after a long and difficult battle. A battle for a better future. A battle for life.

They stopped at the door. Sebastian hugged Angelo. "Do you know who's waiting for you on the other side of the door?"

"Si, Yes," said the boy.

"I'm sure I'll see you around. I live nearby. If you need anything, let me know, ok?"

The boy nodded.

"All right. This is your moment. Here is my phone. Type them a message."

The boy stood silent for a few moments. Then he typed "Hi! I am Angelo. I am outside the door." And he hit send.

# CHAPTER LXV

### *Chanhassen, Minnesota*

When John and Laura opened the door, Sebastian introduced himself as the owner of the Gerard and Sebastian Travels Company, friend of both Lucia Aliberti and Martina Valucelli. Lucia had not provided John and Laura with any information Angelo's journey to the United State, so they had no expectation of his landing in Minneapolis. They had actually thought that Martina was trying to keep him for herself.

Sebastian gave John and Laura the envelope with his and Martina's renunciation to any paternal and maternal rights. Lucia would finalize all the adoption procedures from Italy. He would never forget the scene of love and excitement he had just witnessed. Laura, John and Angelo were all beyond happiness. And yes, the little dog had a good time too. Sebastian was sure that the newly formed family would accept a new, furry addition.

\* \* \*

"Sir, I have a call for you. If you don't mind, I'll activate the car's speaker phone," said the driver.

"Thank you," Sebastian filled a glass of water, to which he added a slice of lemon.

"Good evening Mr. Sebastian, I am Luca, Mr. Marteen and Ms. Valucelli's assistant. I am really sorry to be the person to give you the news, but I am sure both Maarten and Martina would want this to happen this way."

"Sure. Go on."

"The flight you were supposed to be on, had an accident during the landing. One of the wheels took off and the plane completed the landing on its nose. All passengers were affected in one way or another by the accident. But especially passengers in First and Business Class."

"Are you saying that Ms. Valucelli…"

"Yes, Ms. Valucelli is currently in the Emergency Room in Chicago. The driver is taking you to Ms. Valucelli's private Jet which will take you to Chicago. Mr. Robinson and I will be waiting for you at the hospital."

"Of course. I can't even imagine how her husband must be feeling. I'll be honored to join him."

"No, Mr. Sebastian. Ms. Valucelli is not married. Robinson is her real last name. Mr. Robinson is her brother."

Sebastian waited for a moment before replying. "Would his name be Rob, by any chance? Rob Robinson?"

"Yes, he is. I am sending you my phone number via text. Please, call me for anything you may need."

"Thank you. I'll see you in Chicago then."

"Goodbye Sebastian."

"Thank you Luca."

*So Rob is Martina's brother. What if…* Sebastian dialed Fernando's number.

"Fernando. How are you?"

"You crazy Italian! Are you on your way home?"

"No. I'm actually on my way to Chicago."

"Chicago? Have you told Gerard? He is still looking for his phone."

"Fernando, I never asked you. What's the name of your company?"

"If you have not figured it out yet, you will soon. Valucelli Enterprises."

Sebastian hang up the phone and dialed the phone number he had just received via text. "Luca, I need to ask you a crazy question."

"Sure, Mr. Sebastian."

"Are Maarten and Martina related to each other?"

"Well…This is something not many people know…But yes. They are."

"Like...brother and sister?" hinted Sebastian.

"No, Sebastian. Maarten and Martina are the same person. Martina is the glamorous and popular star constantly chased by paparazzi and media. Maarten instead, is a quite low key entrepreneur and benefactor who can live a more open and simple life."

# EPILOGUE

I n a small Minnesota village nestled between cobalt blue waters and emerald woods, a couple, a child sat outside Cafe' Excelsior as their service dog curiously monitored the seagulls chirping around them. The newly-formed family exchanged details on the journey that brought them together. They laughed and they cried. They held each other's hands. They made plans for the future.

Fluffy, white clouds moved eastward lulled by a gentle breeze. When the last puff disappeared in the distant horizon, the family left the table and started walking away. Suddenly, the child stopped and asked something to his mother. She smiled and nodded. She opened her purse and pulled out a small piece of paper, which she handed to her son. He looked at his dog and whispered "andiamo, *let's go!*"

They both sprinted toward the table they had just occupied a few minutes earlier. The boy kissed the small piece of paper and left it on the table. Then he whispered a few words to his dog and they both run back to their parents.

A young man walked toward the table and sat. He looked disheveled and exhausted. For a few minutes he stared at the table. Motionless. Deep in his thoughts. A bartender approached and the two shared a few words. The man picked a piece of paper from the table. It was a small blue business card with a simple tagline embossed in gold *Gerard and Sebastian Travels: What's Your Dream?*

# Acknowledgments

I would like to thank my publisher, Robert Martin, and the team at City Limits Publishing for placing their trust in me and for guiding me as I take my first steps in a new industry. Ever since I was very young, I've always filled notepads and diaries with notes and observations of the places I explored and the people I met. As the years passed, I drafted storylines and characters, but I had no idea of what to do with them. *Angels, Love, and Lost Souls*, the first novel of the 'Gerard and Sebastian Travels' series would have never been possible without the help and guidance of many people.

"Talk a little, listen a lot," my father once told me. And so I did. I was fortunate enough to grow up in a very large family that always maintained strong ties. I can't think of any day that passed by without a large family gathering celebration, a meal with relatives, a trip to visit a distant uncle, a coffee with the elders, or a game of cards at my godparents' home. And all the time I listened – that was easy at a time when diffusion of technology was very limited. I listened to old family tales. I absorbed the constant flow of updates concerning events happening all around Sicily. I hung on to my parents' recollections of war time, their lives as teenagers, or their travels across Italy by car or train in the 60s. Later on, when I left the island to study in the North of Italy, travel across Europe as a member of my University's association of engineers, or for work, I listened to a new group of storytellers: the classmates sharing stories from their homes spread all over Italy, my coworkers in Europe and the United States, the people I met while traveling from one place to the other by train, car, plane, or boat. Thanks to all of you for taking the time to share a moment, a meal, a coffee, a walk in the park with this curious life learner, collector of lifelong friendships. I hope you will find a little piece of you while reading about the journeys that will take Gerard, Sebastian, and their clients meandering around the world.

To the team at Adoption Bridges of Kentucky, to our support group of adoptive families, and to the mothers of our two beautiful children goes my heartfelt thank you. Without you, we would not be the family we are today. The Novel Writing group of brilliant minds who welcomed me with open arms, and is my reliable sounding board for open and constructive feedback. Thank you for your honest guidance. Keep your red ink flowing!

Rick Robinson, mentor and friend. Thank you for your patience and guidance. Our paths crossed many years ago, and you are still guiding through my journey with your wisdom.

My husband William and my children Christian and Valentina are a constant source of encouragement and love. Thank you for allowing me to "disappear" every evening to write about 1,000 words per night.

And finally, thanks to my mum and dad, Vincy and Cosimo, and to my sister Silvia and my niece Guendalina for keeping an eye on me from far away, for your unconditional love, and for always being there for me. Most of all, thank you for allowing me to be me.

# About the Author

Daniele S. Longo is a seasoned traveler and a curious life learner. He lived, worked or travelled in 20+ countries (plus sea), changed job multiple times with 7 different companies and relocated 9 times across Europe and the United States. Avid observer, since he left Sicily, 30 years ago, Daniele has made it his quest to learn as much as possible about the places he explored by visiting unique locations, learning how to cook local dishes, listening to folk stories and music, studying local history, and collecting lifelong friendships worldwide.

Daniele holds a MS in Industrial Engineering (Politecnico di Torino, Italy) and a MBA in Marketing and Entrepreneurship (Northern Kentucky University). For the time being, Daniele lives with his husband, two children and a lovely dog in Chanhassen, Minnesota, where he works in Healthcare and Automation. Passionate about technology, avid reader and collector of old books, he is constantly planning unique journeys for his family and friends.